THE
TASTE OF
NOVA SCOTIA
COOKBOOK

CHARLES LIEF AND HEATHER MacKENZIE

FOREWORD BY ELIZABETH BAIRD

KEY PORTER BOOKS

The publisher gratefully acknowledges the assistance of the Canada
Council and the Ontario Arts Council.

CANADIAN CATALOGUING IN PUBLICATION DATA

Lief, Charles
The taste of Nova Scotia cookbook

Includes index.
ISBN 1-55013-527-9

1. Cookery, Canadian – Nova Scotia style.
2. Cookery – Nova Scotia.   I. MacKenzie, Heather
(Heather Corrine).   II. Title

TX715.6.L54 1994   641.59716   C94-930807-2

Key Porter Books Limited
70 The Esplanade
Toronto, Ontario
Canada M5E 1R2

Design: Scott Richardson
Typesetting: MacTrix DTP
Printed and bound in Canada

94 95 96 97 98 6 5 4 3 2 1

Contents

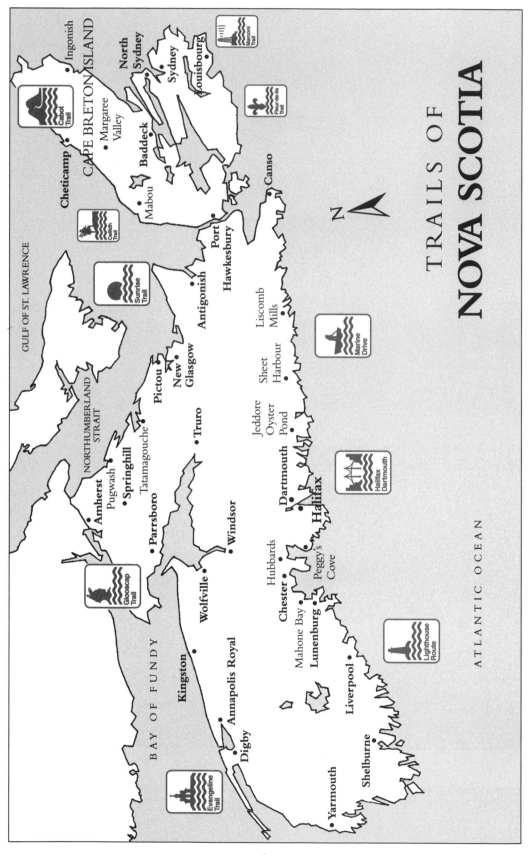

TRAILS OF
NOVA SCOTIA

CAPE BRETON ISLAND

Ingonish

Cabot Trail

Cheticamp

Margaree
Valley

Baddeck

Mabou

Meroni Trail

North
Sydney

Sydney

Louisbourg

Fleur-de-lis Trail

Ceilidh Trail

Port
Hawkesbury

Canso

GULF OF ST. LAWRENCE

Sunrise Trail

Antigonish

N

NORTHUMBERLAND
STRAIT

Pictou

**New
Glasgow**

Liscomb
Mills

Sheet
Harbour

Marine
Drive

Pugwash

Amherst

Springhill

Tatamagouche

Truro

Jeddore
Oyster
Pond

Parrsboro

Windsor

Dartmouth

Glooscap Trail

Halifax
Dartmouth

Halifax

BAY OF FUNDY

Kingston

Wolfville

Hubbards

Chester

Peggy's
Cove

ATLANTIC OCEAN

Annapolis Royal

Mahone Bay

Lunenburg

Lighthouse
Route

Digby

Liverpool

Evangeline
Trail

Yarmouth

Shelburne

TASTING NOVA SCOTIA

REAL TRAVELERS YEARN FOR AN AUTHENTIC EXPERIENCE. THEY WANT TO BIKE THE trails themselves, scout the finest crafts, meander picturesque country villages and fishing towns, and, and this is the biggest "and" of all, taste where they are, savor the place they are visiting.

"Anywhere" North America serves up a steady diet of burgers, fries and pop. Cloned everywhere, for locals and travelers alike. Guaranteed. While this is consoling to some, it's the culinary equivalent of wearing the same clothes as everyone else, day in, day out, forever and ever. Thank goodness there are exceptions to this pervasive assault on variety and difference.

Traveling Nova Scotia is an exception, and a revelation. A fresh introduction to eating, for tired tastebuds. Because in Nova Scotia, good food is alive and well, and comes from the spirit of the people who live here, from the lands they cultivate and the seas they fish.

Helping travelers to discover for themselves the best tastes of this beautiful Atlantic province is an organization called the Taste of Nova Scotia. It's unique in Canada, pulling together agriculture, fisheries and tourism to guide travelers to places where special attention is paid to providing an authentic Nova Scotian food.

Sometimes the experience comes from a kitchen with a sure hand with indigenous ingredients as simple as good homegrown chicken, pearly blue wild blueberries or a Gravenstein apple, crunchy and juicy to bite into. Other times the cooks are offering the right-out-of-the-sea lobster, salmon, mussels visitors are bent on experiencing.

The places to taste this food vary as much as the food itself, from drive-ins to world-class hotels, with many a small inn, smokehouse, bakery, heritage resort and local restaurant in between. But the pledge is the same, Nova Scotian food treated with respect and creativity.

To capture some of these tastes and allow you to create them in your own kitchen is a challenge that *The Taste of Nova Scotia Cookbook* has taken up on the pages that follow. Gathered here are the best recipes from the establishments the Taste of Nova Scotia represents. Some of the dishes, especially ones featuring the all-favorite seafood, are decidedly fancy, perfect for special occasions. Others are as simple and old-fashioned as pickles or homemade bread, memorable for their freshness and quality starter ingredients. All the recipes have been tested to make sure they work in home kitchens, and are arranged in chapters with essays that provide insight into the food highlighted in Nova Scotia and on these pages.

– Elizabeth Baird

ACKNOWLEDGEMENTS

THIS COOKBOOK IN THE SPIRIT OF THE TASTE OF NOVA SCOTIA PROGRAM HAS BEEN a collaboration from beginning to end. The assistance, information, support and advice we received from our member restaurants, the Nova Scotia government, friends, family and foodies across Canada and the United States made the development of our first Taste of Nova Scotia cookbook an exciting and challenging experience.

Once the initial concept of a cookbook celebrating Nova Scotia cuisine was endorsed by our Board of Directors we needed help to write a book which would represent not only the wide variety of food products produced in Nova Scotia but also to convey our rich culture. We would like to acknowledge all those who helped us along the way.

We extend a very special thanks to all our member restaurants, commodity associations, the Nova Scotia Department of Agriculture and Marketing, the Nova Scotia Department of Fisheries, and friends and family who provided us with recipes from their kitchens to be enjoyed in yours. We are grateful to the following recipe contributors:

Amherst Shore Country Inn – Donna Laceby; Bell Buoy Restaurant; Blomidon Inn – Jim Laceby; Blueberry Producers Association of Nova Scotia; Château Halifax; Chez La Vigne – Alex Claval; Crown Bistro Restaurant – Bruno Seiberath; Phyllis Cipolla; Cynthia Driskill; Nova Scotia Fruit

Growers Association; The Galley Seafood Restaurant & Lounge – Janet Hatt; James Gimian; Glenora Inn & Distillery; Granite Brewery; Halliburton House Inn; Keltic Lodge – Gilles Hostel; Larkin's Bake Shop & Café – Francis Larkin-Reynolds; Liscombe Lodge; Markland By The Sea; Normaway Inn – David MacDonald; Paradise Bakery – Norris Eddy; The Pines Resort Hotel – Claude Aucoin; The Prince George Hotel – Steve Huston; Sheep Producers Association of Nova Scotia; Silver Dart Lodge; Silver Spoon Restaurant – Deanna Silver; South Shore Country Inn – Avril Betts; Strawberry Growers Association; Tattingstone Inn – Betsy Harwood; Thackeray's Restaurant & Bar – Les Dowell; Upper Deck Waterfront Fishery & Grill – Alan Johnston; Vegetable and Potato Producers Association of Nova Scotia.

Special thanks to both Linda MacDonald (of the Nova Scotia Department of Agriculture and Marketing) and Ellen O'Reilly (of the Nova Scotia Department of Fisheries) for providing us with food needed by our recipe testers, and also to the Department of Tourism and Culture for their ongoing support of our ideas. We were provided great assistance and expert advice by recipe testers Phyllis Cipolla, Debbie Creelman and Ruth Smith. Dawn Ferguson in the Taste of Nova Scotia office typed and edited our manuscript many times.

Elizabeth Baird, whose cookbook expertise provided us with a guiding hand throughout the process, has been an invaluable and greatly appreciated ally and adviser.

Thanks to our families, Judy, Jessica and Deborah Lief and Les, Joanne and Craig MacKenzie, who encouraged us along the way, ate both the successes and the failures and remained good-humored, even though our second careers as authors took up countless evenings and weekends.

A note of gratitude should be extended to the Board of Directors of Taste of Nova Scotia, which happily invested staff time and program money in this project.

We are particularly grateful to Anna Porter who, after a twenty-minute call from a phone booth at the Halifax airport, expressed considerable enthusiasm in the project. Susan Renouf, the editor-in-chief and Renée Dykeman, our editor, patiently carried two novice authors through the process.

INTRODUCTION

IN THE 1600S, THE PROMISE OF FREEDOM AND ADVENTURE IN THE "NEW WORLD"
began attracting settlers from Europe to North America. Nova Scotia, jutting
out into the Atlantic like the bow of a great ship, became the destination of a
diverse group of European immigrants. They arrived from France, England,
Scotland, Ireland and Germany. During the troubles in the American colonies,
the Europeans were joined by Loyalists who refused to become Americans, and
Black slaves freed by British edict (who created the largest colony of free Blacks
in North America). All of these farmers, fishermen, tradespeople, merchants,
serfs and former slaves arrived to find a sophisticated aboriginal Mi'kmaq culture
which dated back 15,000 years. The twentieth century brought a new wave of
immigration from the Caribbean, Italy, Greece, the Middle East, Southeast Asia
and India.

While the arrival of immigrants to the western hemisphere is not
unique to Nova Scotia, our province has a population of under a million and is
connected to the rest of mainland North America by the thinnest of land bridges.
Our small size, relative isolation and proud ethnic background makes for a
wonderfully rich and diverse heritage, one which is fiercely loyal to its roots.
Language helps preserve culture. In Nova Scotia people speak a variety of
tongues, including Mi'kmaq, French, English, German and Gaelic. We keep
the traditions alive. Nowhere else in North America does the skirl of bagpipes

open a session of the legislature. And only in Nova Scotia can a student attend a Gaelic college.

Maintaining old identities and history while being open to new neighbors with new cultures is not always easy. There is, however, common ground: a natural bounty which is the envy of all who visit Nova Scotia. We are surrounded by a sea rich with lobster, Digby scallops, mussels, crab, clams, cod, herring, halibut, salmon and trout. Our valleys and hillsides nurture dairy cattle, sheep, pigs and chickens. Trees, bushes and vines are laden with apples, blueberries, straw-berries, grapes, pears and countless other fruits, vegetables and grains. The woods offer game, wild mushrooms and the finest maple syrup in the world.

This province, with its beautiful, temperate summers, glorious, golden autumns and cold, pristine winters, provides a backdrop which sparks a creative celebration of food. Our ancestors before us and the professional and non-professional cooks of the present make full use of the harvest of the land and the bounty of the sea. The result is the art of Nova Scotia cooking.

What is Nova Scotia cuisine? We traveled the province asking the chefs at various fine resorts, the cooks at lobster suppers and roadside diners and the food writers and eaters, but no one gave us the same answer. "It's the kind of food my grandmother cooked." "It's the way we use ingredients that are around us." "It's ethnic heritage kept alive through food." "It's simple food . . . fresh food . . . comfort food. . . ." You get the point.

We concluded that the answer is found with each individual. Nova Scotia regional cooking is no different from the cooking found anywhere else in the world. The ingredients vary widely, the tastes, textures and colors change from place to place, but the basics are the same. Honest, full-flavored creations, respecting the heritage of the cooks of our past and the playfulness and skill of those of today.

This cookbook is about the art of cooking as it has developed, and continues to develop, in Nova Scotia. The chefs of our province, some born here and some "from away," have turned their creative minds loose and are using Nova Scotia ingredients to produce delicious colorful and beautifully presented dishes. They have explored and updated traditional recipes served on farms, at church suppers and at the food festivals that take place every year. They have come up with innovative dishes as well, which have impressed visiting world-class chefs, food critics and the hundreds of thousands of tourists who travel to Nova Scotia each year.

The Taste of Nova Scotia is a province-wide restaurant marketing program that was launched in 1989 as a cooperative initiative between the Nova Scotia government and members of the hospitality and food service industry. The goals of the program are twofold: first to enhance the awareness of and increase the use of quality Nova Scotian agricultural and fishery food products through qualifying restaurants; and second, to market Nova Scotia as a destination known for good food and in doing so to reflect the long cultural and culinary history the province has to offer.

Member restaurants of the Taste of Nova Scotia are committed to offering their guests the best food, service and hospitality possible. Each restaurant must apply for membership to the program and meet all its criteria. This commitment to quality is ongoing, and incognito assessments are performed on a regular basis to ensure that standards are maintained. Taste of Nova Scotia member restaurants are listed each year in a Dining Guide that provides the guide user with information on the variety of dining styles represented, a brief description of each property, its specialities, price ranges, hours of operation and other pertinent information.

The Taste of Nova Scotia program works very closely with producers, packers and distributors of Nova Scotian food products, helping to make the connection between producers and users. The program also works with the Nova Scotia Department of Tourism and Culture and the Nova Scotia Department of Agriculture and Marketing, our two government funding partners whose commitment and support of our program has been essential for growth. The Nova Scotia Department of Fisheries, Nova Scotia Restaurant & Food Service Association, Nova Scotia Chef's Association and the Innkeepers Guild of Nova Scotia are also partners in the program. A Taste of Nova Scotia experience is one in which good food, warm atmosphere and sincere service are offered by people who care deeply for their heritage.

The readers of *The Taste of Nova Scotia Cookbook* will journey through the province known as "Canada's Ocean Playground." Hear the voices of the fisherman and the farmer, feel the beauty of the land, and be guided through the preparation of the dishes we are proud to have developed.

For further information on the Taste of Nova Scotia program or to receive our current dining guide listing member restaurants, please contact:

Taste of Nova Scotia
P.O. Box 487
Halifax, Nova Scotia
B3J 2R7

Phone: 902-422-6368
Fax: 902-425-1025

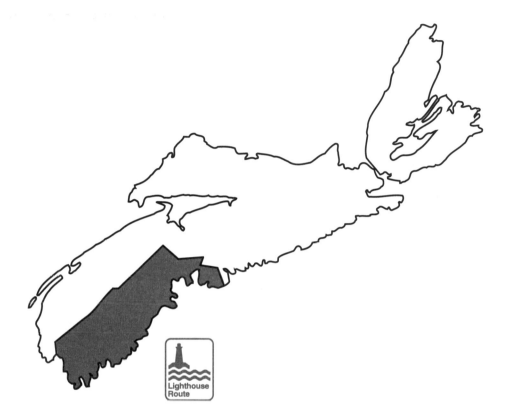

THE LIGHTHOUSE ROUTE

A QUEST FOR INFORMATION ABOUT SMOKED SALMON BROUGHT US TO THE VILLAGE of Seabright, on Nova Scotia's south shore. Our destination, 100 yards past the village sign, was the white building with dark green trim, home of Seabright Smokehouse Ltd. For millions of people around the world a mention of Nova Scotia conjures up tasty memories of smoked salmon (even called "nova" in New England), and Seabright (population 476) is the smoked salmon capital of the province.

Simon Krasemann was unemployed in the early 1980s and, with the entrepreneurial spirit common to Nova Scotians, borrowed $50 and built a smokehouse ("the size of an outhouse"). He bought some salmon from the locals and learned to fillet and completely de-bone the orange-fleshed fish to prepare it for smoking.

We were drinking coffee and eating Kathleen Krasemann's butter tarts while Simon was explaining Seabright Smokehouse's origins. Interrupting the history, we asked a question raised to us by a fan of New York delicatessens — what is the difference between lox and smoked salmon?

Simon said, "Lox was the name of the Scottish technique of heavily salting the salmon before smoking it. The large amount of salt was needed to preserve the fish, in the days before refrigeration. We use salt for flavor, not as a preservative, so our smoked salmon is more delicate, less salty."

With this clarified, we asked Simon to go on. "I experimented with the mix of salt and length of smoking time, until we were happy with the results. I took the fish up and down the road, selling it to neighbors and friends, who seemed to approve."

Today the smokehouse is in a larger building than the original, although still very crowded with the employees and the smokers. The employees are dressed in Helly Hensons, the heavy bright yellow aprons worn by fish processors all over eastern Canada. They wear high rubber boots as well, since despite the delicacy of the finished product the process is messy.

One person fillets the salmon, another de-bones and a third washes the prepared fish, salts it and allows it to rest for eight hours. "This draws out a lot of the moisture so the salmon stays firm when it's smoked," the salter told us. Simon still can fillet and de-bone a salmon twice as fast as most, but business keeps him in the office more and more.

The smokers are stainless steel with small fireboxes that hold smoldering sawdust. The smoke is pulled around the fish by fans at the top. The air above the fish is heated by electric coils, embedded in the smoker box, to dry the fish as it smokes for 10 to 14 hours.

These days wild salmon are very hard to come by. There is no wild salmon commercial fishery in Nova Scotia. Seabright uses farm-raised salmon, which gives Simon the consistent quality and large supply he needs. After the smoker works its magic, the resulting fish is evenly sliced and packaged for sale to the intrepid buyer who makes the trip to the south shore or to a growing list of restaurants and food shops.

This is a labor-intensive process that does not lend itself to mass production. Simon has five employees and now produces up to 800 sides of smoked salmon a week (averaging 300 to 400 sides), sold around the world (there is a growing market in Jordan, we are told). What is received by the consumer is a beautiful burnt-orange fish, which offers a silky, sweet, salty and smoky burst of flavor.

Seabright also smokes scallops, northern shrimp, oysters and the occasional mackerel, but salmon is king. Kathleen tells us that her current favorite way of eating the salmon is with cream cheese and salsa, Nova-Mex cuisine in Seabright.

Seabright is just the beginning of the Lighthouse Route. Farther south, Lunenburg, once the most active fishing port in the Maritimes, is the center of the German culture in Nova Scotia. During the trouble with France in the 1700s, the English government was having difficulty convincing their subjects to settle in Halifax, which they were trying to fortify against a French invasion. They managed to persuade 2400 Germans to move to Halifax, where they were given land to farm. The land wasn't so good and the harbor was tightly controlled by the Royal Navy, so the Germans headed south, and in 1753, along with some Swiss, founded Lunenburg. The land was well suited to farming, and the port was ideal for shipbuilding and as a base for the fishing fleet. They stayed, built and prospered. German was the main language in Lunenburg until well into the 1800s. German food culture influences south shore cooking today, with pickled herring, Lunenburg sausages and meat puddings, sauerkraut and Kohl slaw in abundance.

There are hundreds of hidden harbors and coves all along the Lighthouse Route, which provided a safe haven for pirates and privateers. Mahone Bay was named for the mahonne, a low-lying pirate ship which preyed on the American and European merchant fleets. During the American revolution and the War of 1812 the pirates were called privateers and encouraged by the authorities to continue their careers under the color of the Union Jack. After the wars they became pirates once more.

Oak Island, in Mahone Bay, is said to be a burying place of Bluebeard's fabulous treasure. A "money pit" 100 feet deep and protected by a series of tunnels that could be flooded on cue was discovered in 1795. Despite the planked floors, oak chests and elaborately constructed shafts and tunnels, no pirated gold has been found below the ground. Above the ground is a different story. There is much treasure to be found here, as the residents of the towns and villages, rich in heritage, will agree.

ASPARAGUS WITH APPLE VINAIGRETTE

A platter of bright green asparagus makes a good starter or an elegant addition to the buffet table. This unusual vinaigrette blends the tart and sweet flavors of apple and honey and accents the crisp, earthy taste of the asparagus.

¾ cup	apples, peeled, cored and quartered	175 mL
1 cup	water	250 mL
1 tbsp	honey	15 mL
¼ cup	red wine vinegar	50 mL
½	garlic clove, peeled and minced	½
½-1 tsp	Dijon mustard	2-5 mL
1 tbsp	lemon juice, freshly squeezed	15 mL
1½ tsp	brandy (optional)	7 mL
½ cup	vegetable oil	125 mL
	Salt and pepper	
1½ lb	asparagus, cooked tender crisp	750 g

Vinaigrette: In a saucepan over medium heat, simmer the apples and honey in water until tender. Cool in the pan and remove the apples. Place the apples in a food processor or blender and purée. Add vinegar, garlic, mustard, lemon juice and brandy to the apple purée and blend for one minute. With machine running, add the vegetable oil, blending until smooth. Season with salt and pepper.

Cook or steam asparagus until tender, using one of the methods outlined below. Arrange on individual serving plates and cover with several spoons of vinaigrette.

To cook the asparagus: Wash the stalks to remove any sand. Snap off the tough, woody end. Some people believe in peeling the stalks, but we think that peeling is only useful for thicker stalks that may be a bit over-mature. Cooking time for asparagus depends upon the size of the stalks. Here are two successful methods for cooking fresh asparagus. The first consists of tying the stalks in a bundle with white string. Bring enough salted water to a boil in a deep pot so that the stalks are covered by 4 inches (10 cm) of water when standing upright in the pot. Boil gently for about 7 minutes (for medium-sized stalks). The second method is to set the stalks in a microwave bowl or pan and add about ½ inch (1 cm) of water. Microwave, covered, at full power for 6 minutes.

When cooked, drain and run under cold water to stop the cooking and set the color (of course the cooking methods are good for hot asparagus, too. Just drain and serve, adding some butter, if desired).

Makes 4 servings.

BAKED OYSTERS WITH ARUGULA AND BASIL PESTO

***For an impressive first course, combine this recipe with the following one –
a feast of oysters!***

16	oysters, shucked (reserving the liquor and the bottom shells), Coarse (kosher) salt, sufficient to cover the bottom of a baking sheet	16
2	lemons	2

Arugula and Basil Pesto:

2 tbsp	pine nuts	25 mL
2	cloves garlic, peeled and minced	2
3 cups	arugula leaves, rinsed and dried	750 mL
½ cup	fresh basil leaves	125 mL
½ cup	olive oil	125 mL
	Salt and pepper	
½ cup	freshly grated Parmesan cheese	125 mL

To shuck oysters: Scrub the oysters thoroughly with a stiff brush under cold running water. Hold each oyster in a dish towel in the palm of the hand with the hinged end away from you. Force an oyster knife between the shells at the hinged end, pressing down on the knife to pop open the shell; slide the blade against the flat upper shell to cut the large muscle and free the upper shell. If the shell crumbles and cannot be opened at the hinge, insert the knife between the shells at the curved end of the oyster; pry the shells open and sever the large muscle. Break off and discard the upper shell and slide the knife under the oyster to release it from the bottom shell. Take the reserved liquor, strain it into a bowl through a double thickness of cheesecloth and set aside.

Pesto: In a blender or food processor, process the pine nuts and garlic until finely chopped. Add the arugula and basil leaves and blend until mixture becomes a paste. Add the olive oil slowly, while blending. Remove pesto mixture to a bowl and add the Parmesan cheese, 2 tbsp (25 mL) of the reserved oyster liquor and salt and pepper to taste. (The texture is better if cheese is stirred in by hand.)

Place the salt in an even layer on the baking sheet and set the bottom shells of the oysters on the salt. This prevents the shell from tipping. Place an oyster into each shell and spoon a bit of remaining reserved liquor on the oyster. Bake in a preheated 400°F (200°C) oven for 10 minutes, until cooked through.

Set three oysters on each plate, using some more salt under the oyster for balance, if required. Spoon pesto onto each oyster, squeeze on a bit of lemon juice and serve.

Makes 4 servings.

OYSTERS ON THE HALF-SHELL WITH MIGNONETTE SAUCE

36	oysters, shucked (reserving the liquor)	36
	Mignonette Sauce:	
2 tbsp	minced shallots	25 mL
⅓ cup	red wine vinegar	75 mL
2 tbsp	balsamic vinegar	25 mL
2 tsp	fresh dill, chopped	10 mL
	Freshly ground black pepper	
2 tbsp	olive oil	25 mL
3	lemons, cut into wedges	3

Strain the oyster liquor through a double thickness of cheesecloth into a bowl and reserve. Just before serving, spoon it over the oysters, which have been returned to their bottom shell.

Mignonette sauce: In a bowl, combine shallots, vinegars, dill, pepper and olive oil, mix well, cover and chill until serving time.

Arrange on individual serving plates (using coarse salt spread on the plate to prevent the shells from tipping); spoon some of the mignonette sauce over each and garnish with lemon wedges.

Makes 6 servings.

STEAMED MUSSELS

Nova Scotia is a leader in cultivating mussels, ensuring that a good supply of high-quality shellfish is available all year. This inexpensive relative of the clam is very versatile — served steamed in the shell, broiled on the half-shell or combined in pasta dishes or seafood salads. Some say that wild mussels are more flavorful, but we think the difference is too subtle to notice. Cultivated mussels are graded by size and need only a rinse to clean.

When buying mussels make sure that they smell sweet and "oceany." If you cannot use the mussels right away, they can be stored for 5 to 8 days in the refrigerator. Keep them moist by covering them with a wet cloth or damp newspaper — make sure the air can get to them. Do not keep them in water as they will not live in fresh water and will spoil quickly. Before steaming, remove the "beards" clinging to the shells and tap the shells of any that are not tightly closed. If they do not close, discard them.

Serve steamed mussels in a large bowl with some of the broth from the steaming. Grind some pepper over the top. You can include lemon wedges, melted butter or garlic butter as accompaniments. Set some empty bowls on the table for the shells.

¼ cup	butter	50 mL
1	garlic clove, minced	1
¼ cup	onions, diced	50 mL
¼ cup	celery, diced	50 mL
¼ cup	white wine or water	50 mL
2	bay leaves	2
2 lb	mussels, scrubbed, with beards removed	1 kg
¼ cup	fresh parsley, chopped	50 mL

In a deep saucepan, sauté garlic and onion in melted butter until onions are translucent. Add celery, wine and bay leaves and cook for an additional 2 minutes. Add mussels and cook closely covered on high heat for 6 to 8 minutes or until the mussel shells have opened. Discard any unopened mussels.

Place cooked mussels in a heated serving bowl and pour cooking juice over the top. Garnish with parsley.

Makes 3 to 4 servings.

SMOKED SALMON

Millions of people in the world enjoy smoked salmon, or lox, and call it "nova" without knowing the origin of the word. The smoking style preferred by these deli lovers was perfected in Nova Scotia. If you want the best quality, look for firm-fleshed smoked Atlantic salmon that is not too thinly sliced.

4 oz	smoked salmon, sliced	125 g
4 oz	cream cheese	125 g
1	medium red onion	1
1 tbsp	capers	15 mL
	Freshly ground black pepper	
	Sprigs of fresh dill	
	Thin slices of dark bread	
1	lemon, cut in wedges	1

On a small plate, arrange three or four slices of smoked salmon. Place 1-2 tbsp (15-25 mL) of cream cheese on the side of each plate. Peel and slice the red onion, separating it into rings. Arrange the onion rings on the salmon slices, along with a sprinkle of capers. Grind some pepper over the salmon, garnish with a sprig of fresh dill and serve accompanied by a slice of dark bread. Squeeze some lemon juice over the salmon just before serving.

Makes 4 to 6 servings.

SMOKED SALMON PÂTÉ

This terrific salmon pâté offers an economical and inventive way of serving smoked salmon, either as an informal appetizer with drinks or as an elegant first course. The caviar (even an inexpensive variety) makes the dish that much more impressive. If you can handle the praise, buy small jars of black, red and golden caviar and set a spoonful of each on three dollops of sour cream.

½ cup	unsalted butter	125 mL
⅓ cup	onion, peeled and chopped	75 mL
2	large, fresh basil leaves, torn into small pieces or ½ tsp (2 mL) dried basil	2
½ lb	smoked salmon	250 g
½ lb	cream cheese	250 g
1-2 oz	blue cheese, crumbled (to taste)	30-60 g

In a heavy saucepan over medium heat, melt 2 tbsp (25 mL) butter. Sauté onion until soft; add the remaining butter, basil and smoked salmon. Cook over medium heat until the salmon flakes. Add cream cheese and blue cheese. Cover the saucepan and simmer slowly over low heat for 15 minutes, stirring occasionally to prevent burning. Remove from heat.

Purée the salmon mixture in a food processor until smooth. For best results, add a small amount at a time to ensure the salmon is well puréed. Pour into a non-reactive (i.e., not aluminum) loaf pan and chill for three hours.

Serve with crackers, French bread or on a potato pancake. (To make the potato pancake, grate one raw potato, squeeze out the moisture, form into a pancake and sauté in a non-stick pan with a little melted butter, until both sides are golden brown and crisp.) Garnish with sour cream, a sprinkle of caviar and a fresh sprig of dill.

SPINACH GNOCCHI

*Gnocchi are light dumplings that can be made from wheat flour, nut flour
(such as chestnut) or potato flour. This variety, using all-purpose wheat flour, is flecked
with the bright green spinach, and accented by the red sauce. Gnocchi make a
good first course which could be followed by a fish or chicken dish.*

1½ cups	all-purpose wheat flour	375 mL
pinch	each of salt, pepper and nutmeg	pinch
4	eggs	4
¾ cup	milk	175 mL
⅓ cup	unsalted butter	75 mL
3½ cups	fresh bread crumbs	875 mL
1 tbsp	parsley, chopped	15 mL
1 tbsp	chives, chopped	15 mL
1 cup	spinach, cooked and chopped	250 mL
½ cup	Parmesan cheese, freshly grated	125 mL

In a mixing bowl, combine flour, seasonings, eggs and milk to make a light dough.
In a saucepan over medium heat, melt half of the butter and stir in the bread crumbs.
Continue cooking until the bread crumbs are golden brown, then add the parsley,
chives and spinach. Add bread crumb and spinach mixture to dough and mix well.
Refrigerate dough for one hour.

To shape the dough into a gnocchi or dumpling, use two metal tablespoons. Use one
tablespoon to hold a spoonful of dough; use the second tablespoon to shape the gnocchi.
Drop each gnocchi into a large saucepan of boiling salted water. The dumpling will
float to the surface when cooked; remove from the water with a slotted spoon and
place on a lightly buttered plate. Sprinkle with the freshly grated Parmesan cheese.
In a small saucepan, heat the remaining butter until it bubbles and starts to brown,
then pour over the gnocchi. Top with tomato coulis.

Makes 8 servings.

Tomato Coulis:

1	onion, peeled	1
2	garlic cloves	2
6	fresh basil leaves	6
1	white of small leek, thinly sliced	1
⅓ cup	whipping cream	75 mL
1 lb	ripe tomatoes, peeled, juice squeezed out and diced	500 g
	Salt and pepper	

Chop onion, garlic and basil finely. In a small saucepan, add leek, onion, garlic, basil and cream. Cover and cook over medium heat for 10 minutes. Add tomatoes and cook an additional 5 minutes. Transfer to food processor and purée; season with salt and pepper to taste.

MUSSEL-STUFFED MUSHROOM CAPS

Mushroom caps, commonly stuffed with a bread crumb and cheese mixture, are common hors d'oeuvres. This variation offers an interesting twist by using the chewy texture and maritime flavor of mussels to complement the woodsy mushroom.

1 tbsp	butter or margarine	15 mL
2 tbsp	lemon juice	25 mL
12	large mushroom caps	12
12	mussels, cooked and shucked*	12
3	slices bacon, partially cooked and cut in 1-inch (2.5-cm) pieces	3

In a skillet over medium heat, melt butter, add lemon juice and sauté mushrooms for 3 to 5 minutes. Place mushrooms on a baking sheet; reserve cooking juices. On each inverted mushroom cap, place a mussel and top with a piece of bacon. Pour reserved butter and lemon juices over mussels. Bake in a preheated 450°F (230°C) oven for 10 minutes. Serve hot.

* *To cook mussels, first rinse and inspect them, removing any beard that still remains with either scissors or a quick tug. Place mussels in a pot with ½ cup (125 mL) of water or white wine. Cover and steam over medium heat for 5 to 10 minutes or until shells are open wide and the meat loosens from the shell. Discard any unopened mussels.*

Makes 12 servings.

Asparagus Vichyssoise with Blueberry Sherbet

Cream- or milk-based soups have become less popular lately, because of concern about dietary fat. But if they are served as the center of a light meal, accompanied by a salad and bread, or in smaller portions as a starter, there is certainly still a place for these delicious and comforting soups.

This soup with its bright flavors and pastel colors is a refreshing herald of spring. The soup was created to serve cold, but if the weather is not so springlike, it's a great hot soup (but make sure the sherbet garnish is really firm and place it on the soup just before serving).

1 tbsp	butter	15 mL
¼ cup	onions, peeled and coarsely chopped	50 mL
2½ cups	asparagus, washed, trimmed and cut in 1-inch (2.5-cm) pieces	625 mL
1 cup	potatoes, peeled and cut in ¼-inch (0.6-cm) pieces	250 mL
1 cup	chicken stock	250 mL
2 cups	whipping cream (or milk)	500 mL
1 cup	plain yogurt	250 mL
	White pepper to taste	
½ cup	blueberry or raspberry sherbet	125 mL
	Fresh dill sprigs	

In a saucepan over medium heat, melt the butter and sauté onions, asparagus and potatoes until the onions are translucent. Add chicken stock and 1 cup (250 mL) cream or milk and simmer until vegetables are tender. Season with white pepper to taste. Purée mixture in a food processor or blender until smooth, then pass purée through a very fine sieve or strainer, using the back of a spoon to help push liquid through. When mixture has cooled, add plain yogurt and the other cup of cream or milk, blending well. At this point the soup may be reheated over medium heat, or chilled for 4 hours if serving cold. Garnish each serving with 1 tbsp (15 mL) of sherbet (see recipe on p. 115) and dill sprigs.

Makes 5 to 6 servings.

FIDDLEHEAD SOUP

Here is a simple soup that features the fiddlehead, which is the unopened frond of the ostrich fern. Fiddleheads are now widely available, either fresh in the spring or frozen year round. The flavors of fiddleheads and onions complement each other well, especially when the two are sautéed together.

1 lb	fiddleheads*	500 g
⅓ cup	onions, peeled and diced	75 mL
¼ cup	butter	50 mL
2	medium potatoes, peeled and diced	2
1½ tsp	ground nutmeg	7 mL
5	cups chicken stock	1.2 L
1 cup	whipping cream or milk	250 mL
	Salt and pepper	

Remove the papery outer layer from the fresh fiddleheads, and wash well. In a saucepan over medium heat, melt the butter and sauté the fiddleheads and onions. Add the diced potatoes, nutmeg and chicken stock. Let simmer until potatoes are tender. Remove from heat and purée in processor or blender; strain through a strainer or sieve, and return to heat. Add cream or milk and season to taste.

* *Two packages of frozen fiddleheads (300 g each), thawed and drained, may be substituted.*

Makes 6 to 8 servings.

BROCCOLI APPLE SOUP

This soup is meant to be thick and is very satisfying on a cool day.
Use both the florets and a good bit of the peeled stem of the broccoli to
get a nice thick soup. The apple lends sweetness.

5 cups	broccoli, uncooked, coarsely chopped florets and peeled stems included	1250 mL
3 tbsp	unsalted butter	45 mL
1	small onion, peeled and thinly sliced	1
3	tart apples (Gravenstein or Cortland), peeled, cored and sliced	3
2 cups	chicken stock (broth)	500 mL
¼ cup	crème fraîche, sour cream or plain yogurt	50 mL
2 tbsp	snipped chives	25 mL

Steam broccoli just until tender and set aside. Melt butter in heavy soup pot and sauté the onions and apples until onions are soft but not brown. Add chicken broth and simmer 20 minutes. Remove from heat and strain liquid; set aside. Purée the broccoli, apple and onion in food processor or blender. Transfer liquid and purée back into soup pot and slowly reheat. Place into soup bowls and garnish with a generous spoonful of crème fraîche, sour cream or plain yogurt and snipped chives.

Crème fraîche: Crème fraîche is a wonderful, tart substitute for whipping cream, good for garnishing soups or desserts. It can be found in many markets, but is easy to make at home. To make your own, simply combine 1 cup (250 mL) of whipping cream and 1 tablespoon (15 mL) of buttermilk in a bowl, cover and let stand in a warm place in the kitchen for 12-24 hours until the mixture has thickened. It will keep a week in the refrigerator.

Makes 4 servings.

CARROT PARSNIP BISQUE

*Root vegetables are wonderfully sweet when cooked slowly. Often the
flavor of parsnips is compared to that of carrots, but in this soup each vegetable shines
through distinctly. The acidic bite of the orange adds just the right zip.*

¼ cup	butter	50 mL
2	medium onions, peeled and chopped	2
2	large potatoes, peeled and diced	2
4	carrots, peeled and diced	4
4	parsnips, peeled and diced	4
4 cups	chicken stock (broth)	1 L
½ tsp	ground nutmeg	2 mL
2 tbsp	lemon juice	25 mL
2 tbsp	orange juice, freshly squeezed	25 mL
⅓ cup	10% cream or whole milk	75 mL
	Salt and pepper	
	Zest of one orange, finely chopped	
	(for garnish)	

In medium saucepan over moderately low heat, melt butter and cook the onions,
potatoes, carrots and parsnips for 10 minutes, stirring occasionally. Add the stock and
simmer for 20 minutes or until vegetables are tender. In a blender or food processor,
purée the mixture until smooth. Return to the saucepan and add nutmeg, juices and
the cream or milk. Heat over medium low heat until hot and serve in bowls, sprinkling
the orange zest on top before serving.

Make 4 to 6 servings.

CURRIED PUMPKIN AND MUSHROOM SOUP

In the autumn the fields of Nova Scotia are bright orange with ripe pumpkins.
Pies and jack-o'-lanterns are not the only uses for this sweet, smooth-fleshed vegetable.
This soup is hearty and the mushrooms add a pleasing depth of flavor.
Wild mushrooms such as boletus or the imperial matsutake will add even
more taste. Float some sautéed slices of mushroom on top.

¾ lb	mushrooms, thinly sliced	375 g
1½ cups	onions, chopped	375 mL
3 tbsp	butter	45 mL
3 tbsp	all-purpose flour	45 mL
1½ tbsp	curry powder	20 mL
4 cups	chicken stock	1 L
4 cups	pumpkin, puréed*	1 L
3 tbsp	brown sugar	45 mL
½ tsp	nutmeg	2 mL
3 cups	whipping cream	750 mL
	Sour cream	

In a large saucepan over medium heat, sauté mushrooms and onions in butter until onions are translucent. Add flour and curry powder and blend, stirring for 5 minutes. Add chicken stock, pumpkin, brown sugar and nutmeg, stirring until blended. Transfer to food processor or blender and purée until smooth. Add cream. Return to saucepan and reheat until hot. Serve hot with a dollop of sour cream and nutmeg.

* Pumpkin can be purchased in cans at the supermarket or you can make your own puréed pumpkin at home. Take a medium-sized pumpkin and cut into wedges, approximately 1 inch (2.5 cm) thick. Seed, peel and cut into cubes. Place in a large stockpot and cover with water and bring to a boil, reduce heat and cook until the pumpkin is tender. Drain the pumpkin in a colander. Place well-drained pumpkin in a food processor or blender and purée until smooth. This purée also works well as a base for pumpkin pie or cheesecake. The same method can be used for puréed squash, which will also work in this recipe.

Makes 8 to 10 servings.

STRAWBERRY SOUP

Every year it's the same thing — winter stays longer than it should and gives way to a cold, damp spring. Just when the complaints about the weather are at their peak, an explosion of sunshine and warmth overtakes the province and strawberry blossoms carpet the fields. This smooth soup is what summer is all about.

6 cups	fresh whole strawberries	1.5 L
	(or frozen, thawed and drained)	
½ cup	granulated sugar	125 mL
¼ cup	liquid honey	50 mL
1 cup	strawberry yogurt	250 mL
¾ cup	cold water	175 mL
1½ tsp	lemon juice, freshly squeezed	7 mL
¼ tsp	salt	1 mL
⅓ cup	port (optional)	75 mL

Wash and hull fresh strawberries. Combine strawberries, sugar, honey and yogurt in food processor and blend until smooth. Add water, lemon juice, salt and port to strawberry mixture and blend thoroughly. Refrigerate for several hours to blend flavors before serving. Serve soup in chilled bowl, garnished with a strawberry slice and fresh mint leaf.

Makes 6 servings.

LIMA BEAN AND VEGETABLE SOUP

Soup does not need to be cream based to be hearty and satisfying. Lima beans and winter vegetables join to create a soup that is a filling meal with the addition of some bread and butter. As with many bean-based soups, this one is even better a day or two after it was first made. Reheated, the flavors blend even more thoroughly.

1 cup	dry lima beans	250 mL
10 cups	water	2.5 L
1	bay leaf	1
1½ tsp	salt	7 mL
3 tbsp	butter	45 mL
1	onion, peeled and diced	1
½ tsp each	dried thyme, marjoram, summer savory	2 mL each
2	cloves garlic, finely chopped	2
1	12-oz (341-mL) can plum tomatoes	1
½ cup	dry white wine (optional)	125 mL
2	medium carrots, peeled and cut into ½-inch (1-cm) pieces	2
1	small turnip, peeled and cut into ½-inch (1-cm) pieces	1
¼ lb	mushrooms, chopped	125 g
2	medium potatoes, peeled and cut into ½-inch (1-cm) pieces	2
4 cups	chicken or vegetable stock	1 L
4 cups	bean broth	1 L
	Freshly ground pepper	
	Freshly grated Parmesan cheese (optional)	

Rinse the beans, then drain. In a mixing bowl, soak the beans in 2 cups (500 mL) of water for 6 hours or overnight, then drain. In a large soup pot, add drained beans, bay leaf and 8 cups (2 L) water. Bring to a boil and add 1 tsp (5 mL) salt. Lower heat and simmer until the beans are about tender. Drain, reserving broth for later use.

In a large soup pot, melt the butter, add the onion and cook over medium heat, stirring frequently, until the onion turns a deep golden brown, about 10 to 15 minutes. Add salt, thyme, marjoram, summer savory, garlic and tomatoes. Cook for 2 minutes, add the wine and cook an additional 2 minutes. Add the carrots, turnip, mushrooms, potatoes, chicken stock and reserved bean broth. Cook at a lively simmer for 15 minutes, add the beans and cook another 30 minutes. Season with salt and pepper to taste.

Garnish if desired with some freshly grated Parmesan cheese.

Makes 8 servings.

HARVEST SOUP

Midway through the summer gardening season, a variety of vegetables are mature enough to be harvested together. They can be combined in a fresh, meatless soup that highlights the sweet freshness of the produce. This Harvest Soup recipe features carrots, zucchini, snow peas and cherry tomatoes. As the summer months progress, new combinations can be created using the same basic approach.

2 tbsp	vegetable oil	25 mL
2	cloves garlic, minced	2
1 cup	baby carrots, whole or halved	250 mL
1 cup	zucchini, quartered, seeded and sliced	250 mL
1 cup	snow peas, halved	250 mL
1 cup	cherry tomatoes, halved	250 mL
½ cup	green onion, chopped	125 mL
1 tbsp	dried basil	15 mL
1 tsp	dried tarragon	5 mL
6 cups	water	1.5 L
	Salt and pepper	

In a large saucepan or soup pot, heat oil over medium heat. Add garlic, carrots, zucchini, peas, tomatoes and green onions and sauté for 5 to 7 minutes. Add basil, tarragon and water. Simmer for 15 minutes or until vegetables are tender crisp. Season with salt and pepper to taste.

Makes 6 servings.

FISH STOCK

A good fish stock is a central element in sauces and soups with Maritime roots. The stock is easy to make and can be frozen. There are countless variations on the basic recipe, but we find this to be one of the most versatile.

3 tbsp	butter	45 mL
½ cup	onions, peeled and chopped	125 mL
¼ cup	carrots, peeled and chopped	50 mL
½ cup	celery, chopped	125 mL
6	white peppercorns	6
3-4	whole cloves	3-4
½ cup	white wine	125 mL
2 cups	cold water	500 mL
2 tbsp	fresh parsley, chopped	25 mL
1	bay leaf	1
1 tsp	dried thyme (use 1 tbsp or or 15 mL chopped if fresh)	5 mL
1 tsp	dried marjoram (use 1 tbsp or 15 mL chopped if fresh)	5 mL
	Zest of one lemon	
1½ lb	white fish, cut into pieces*	750 g

In a saucepan over medium heat, melt butter, add onions, carrots and celery, and simmer for 5 minutes. Add peppercorn, cloves, wine, water, parsley, bay leaf, thyme, marjoram and lemon zest, and stir. Add fish and simmer for 20 to 30 minutes, seasoning to taste with salt and pepper. Strain the mixture through a fine sieve. This gives you a clean stock that can be used in sauces, as a base for many soups, for steaming mussels or as a poaching liquid for fish. The stock will keep for several days in the refrigerator or for 3 to 4 weeks in the freezer.

* Any inexpensive white-fleshed fish is suitable for this mild fish stock, such as cusk or ocean perch. Use the whole fish, including heads and tails if you can.

Note: If a stronger-flavored fish stock is needed for your recipe, add ½ cup (125 mL) of clam juice.

Makes 2 cups (500 mL).

LOBSTER CHOWDER

This is a rich chowder packed with plenty of lobster. It can be served in small cups for a very special first course or in larger bowls as the centerpiece of an informal supper. The sour cream adds an unexpected and delicious tartness.

1⅔ cups	potatoes, peeled and diced	400 mL
2 tbsp	butter	25 mL
1½ cups	onions, peeled and minced finely	375 mL
2 tbsp	dried thyme leaves	25 mL
1½ tsp	celery salt	7 mL
¼ tsp	black pepper	1 mL
¾ cup	sour cream	175 mL
1½ cup	whipping cream	375 mL
1 cup	milk	250 mL
2 cups	lobster meat, cooked and chopped, plus juices*	500 mL

Steam the potatoes in a saucepan for 8 minutes, remove from heat and set aside. In a large saucepan over medium heat, sauté onions in butter until soft and transparent; do not overcook. Stir in the thyme, celery salt and pepper, and then the potatoes. Blend the sour cream, whipping cream, milk and the lobster meat and juice. Heat through, but do not boil.

* *An 11-oz (312-mL) tin of frozen lobster may be substituted.*

Makes 6 servings.

Nova Scotia Bouillabaisse

This soup, with its light tomato-based broth, allows the pure flavors of the seafood to burst through, and makes a nice change from creamy chowders. Top-quality ingredients are the key to success here. If you can't get really fresh seafood, use well-prepared frozen fish.

2 tbsp	vegetable oil	25 mL
½ cup	onions, peeled and chopped	125 mL
3	garlic cloves, crushed	3
1½ cup	Clamato juice	375 mL
1	12-oz (341-mL) tin whole, peeled tomatoes, undrained	1
½ tsp	orange peel, grated	2 mL
½ tsp	salt	2 mL
¼ tsp	saffron threads	1 mL
¼ tsp	fennel seed	1 mL
⅛ tsp	dried thyme	0.5 mL
⅛ tsp	pepper	0.5 mL
1	bay leaf	1
¾-1 lb	lobster meat	350–500 g
½ lb	haddock or cod	250 g
½ lb	halibut	250 g
¼ lb	scallops	125 g
8	mussels or clams, in shells, cleaned	8

Heat oil in saucepan. Sauté chopped onions and garlic until onions are tender. Stir in Clamato juice, undrained tomatoes, orange peel, salt, saffron, fennel, thyme, pepper and bay leaf and bring to a boil. Reduce heat and simmer mixture, covered, for 20 minutes. Meanwhile, prepare lobster, haddock and halibut by cutting into ½-inch (1-cm) pieces. Add to tomato mixture, along with scallops and mussels. Simmer for 10 minutes or until mussels open (seafood is usually added about 10 minutes before serving to ensure that the fish is not overcooked).

Makes 4 servings.

SEAFOOD CHOWDER

A lunch of hot chowder and fresh rolls, eaten on a deck or dining room overlooking the ocean, is often one of the fondest memories that visitors have of Nova Scotia. As you can imagine, chowder recipes are numerous and often well-guarded secrets. The first one, from Cape Breton, uses scallops, salmon and mussels in a contemporary version of the Nova Scotia classic. The second one is rich with cream and is very traditional. Do not overcook the fish.

¼ cup	butter	50 mL
3	potatoes, diced	3
2	stalks celery, diced	2
1	carrot, diced	1
1	onion, diced	1
1	clove garlic, minced	1
¼ cup	all-purpose flour	50 mL
6 cups	chicken or fish stock	1.5 L
½ lb	boneless, skinless salmon, cubed	250 g
¼ lb	scallops, sliced	125 g
1 lb	mussels, scrubbed	500 g
¼ cup	whipping cream	50 mL
4 tsp	each of fresh dill and basil, chopped	20 mL
¼ tsp	pepper	1 mL

In a large heavy saucepan, melt butter over medium-high heat; cook potatoes, celery, carrot, onion and garlic, stirring, for 8 minutes or until softened. Stir in flour. Gradually whisk in 5 cups (1.25 L) of the stock; bring to a boil. Reduce heat and simmer, covered, for about 10 minutes or until vegetables are tender.

Meanwhile, in a separate saucepan, bring remaining stock to a boil. Reduce heat to simmer and poach salmon for 1 minute; remove with slotted spoon and set aside. Poach scallops for 1 minute; add to salmon. Poach mussels, covered, for 3 minutes or until mussels open; add to salmon, discarding any mussels that do not open.

Strain poaching liquid into vegetable mixture. Add cream, dill, basil and pepper; heat through. Add reserved seafood; heat through until steaming.

Makes 6 servings.

NOVA SCOTIA SEAFOOD CHOWDER

⟩	2 cups	lobster meat	500 mL
1/2	1 lb	fish fillets (haddock, cod, halibut, etc.)	500 g
1/4	½ cup	onions, chopped	125 mL
1/8	¼ cup	butter or margarine	50 mL
1	2 tbsp	all-purpose flour	25 mL
2	4 cups	potatoes, peeled and diced	1 L
1/2	1 cup	water	250 mL
1/2	1 lb	scallops	500 g
2	4 cups	10% cream	1 L
1.5	3 cups	milk	750 g
1/2	1 tsp	salt	5 mL
	pinch	white cayenne pepper	pinch
1/2	1 lb	mussels or clams, steamed and shucked	500 g

If frozen, thaw lobster, reserving the lobster juice. Remove any bits of shell or cartilage and cut into bite-size pieces. De-bone fish fillets and cut into 1-inch (2-cm) pieces. Set aside.

In a heavy saucepan, sauté onions in butter until tender. Stir in flour and cook for 1 minute. Add potatoes and enough water to cover, bring to a boil, cook until tender. Add fish, scallops, and simmer for 5 minutes, stirring once or twice. Add cream, milk, lobster, lobster juice, mussels and seasonings. Heat gently and serve.

Makes 12 servings.

$\frac{1}{2}$

APPLE AND PEAR SALAD

This salad is a crunchy combination of Nova Scotia's two premier fall fruits. It would make a delicious lunch accompanied by some fresh tuna or chicken salad, and served with a multigrain bread or roll. There are many varieties of apples and pears from which to choose. Cortland, Gravenstein, Spartan or Northern Spy are excellent salad apples. Bartlett pears are a good pear variety.

2	red apples, unpeeled	2
2	pears, peeled	2
2 tbsp	lemon juice, freshly squeezed	25 mL
¼ cup	mayonnaise	50 mL
¼ cup	plain yogurt	50 mL
3 cups	cabbage, coarsely shredded	750 mL
¼ cup	celery, chopped	50 mL
¼ cup	onion, peeled and chopped	50 mL
¼ cup	pecans or walnuts, chopped	50 mL
¼ cup	raisins	50 mL
	Salt and pepper	

Core and dice one apple and one pear, then toss with lemon juice. Set aside. Blend mayonnaise and yogurt until smooth. In a bowl, combine cabbage, celery, onion, nuts and raisins; add in apple and pear. Add mayonnaise and yogurt dressing, tossing until all ingredients are well coated. Season with salt and pepper to taste. Chill for at least one hour before serving, to blend flavors. Garnish with fresh apple and pear slices.

Makes 6 servings.

PASTA SALAD WITH CHANTERELLE DRESSING

Pasta, in great varieties of shapes and sizes, is the most popular food offering of the Italian community in Nova Scotia. This salad takes advantage of the summer harvest of tomatoes, snow peas, fresh herbs and woodland treasure of chanterelle mushrooms.

Dressing:

1 oz	fresh chanterelles	30 g
	(½ oz or 15 g if dried)	
1½ tsp	shallots, finely chopped	7 mL
1½ tsp	olive oil	7 mL
1 tbsp	fresh basil, chopped or	15 mL
	½ tsp (2 mL) dried	
½ tsp	Dijon mustard	2 mL
2 tbsp	wine vinegar	25 mL
1 tbsp	balsamic vinegar	15 mL
½ cup	vegetable or walnut oil	125 mL
	Salt and freshly ground pepper	

Pasta Salad:

½ lb	dried rotini or fusilli pasta	250 g
½	medium red pepper, roasted	½
¼ lb	cherry tomato, stems removed	125 g
¼ lb	snow peas, sliced into 1-inch	125 g
	(2.5-cm) pieces	
¼ cup	pitted black olives, chopped	50 mL
1	head of Boston or other soft lettuce	1

Dressing: This dressing is best made the day before serving, to allow the flavors to blend. If using dried chanterelles, place in a small bowl with wine and balsamic vinegars and soak for 1 to 2 hours or until mushrooms soften. Drain and reserve the vinegar. If using fresh chanterelles, wipe clean and cut large mushrooms into 1-inch (2.5-cm) pieces, leaving smaller ones whole.

Heat the olive oil in a skillet over medium heat. Add the shallots, cooking until they are translucent. Add the chanterelles and increase the heat, cook for a minute, stirring to cook mushrooms evenly. In a mixing bowl, combine basil, mustard, vinegars, oil, and salt and pepper, whisk to blend. Add mushroom mixture and whisk thoroughly. Cover and refrigerate for at least 12 hours to allow flavors to blend.

Pasta Salad: Cook pasta in salted boiling water until just tender (about 10 to 12 minutes). Drain the pasta and cover with cold water to stop the cooking; drain again when cool. Place pasta in a large bowl.

To roast pepper, preheat the broiler and place the pepper on a broiling pan about 2 inches (5 cm) from the flame. Broil, turning as needed, until the skin is charred and blistered all around. Place the pepper into a paper bag and twist the top closed, allowing the pepper to cool in the bag for 10 minutes. When cool, remove the pepper and peel off the skin by hand – it will come off easily. Remove the seeds and chop the pepper. Add the pepper, tomatoes, peas and olives to the pasta. Give the chanterelle dressing another whisk and add to pasta mixture. Stir to coat with dressing.

Line a plate with lettuce and serve salad on top.

Makes 8 servings.

CUCUMBER SALAD

This salad is particularly refreshing served right from the refrigerator. It makes a good accompaniment to smoked fish, pickled herring or sliced cold pork.

3-4	cucumbers	3-4
1	onion, peeled and chopped	1
	Salt	
1 cup	sour cream	250 mL
1 tbsp	white vinegar	15 mL
3 tbsp	granulated sugar	45 mL
	Freshly ground pepper	

Peel and thinly slice cucumbers. In a large bowl, combine cucumbers and onion slices in alternating layers, starting with cucumbers. Sprinkle each layer with salt. Place a weighted plate on top, touching the vegetables, and press for several hours.

Prepare dressing by combining sour cream, vinegar and sugar, blending until smooth, and then refrigerate. Drain vegetables well (rinse with cold water, if desired, to remove excess salt, then drain). Combine sour cream mixture with vegetables, stirring to coat well. Grind some pepper over top just before serving.

Makes 8 servings.

GREEN BEAN, TOMATO AND ENDIVE SALAD WITH GOAT CHEESE TOAST

A perfect salad to make after a trip to the farmers' market, where all of the ingredients (except olive oil) are local. This is a summer salad that is best when made with vine-ripened tomatoes. The idea of using warmed goat cheese on the salad comes from the French.

Salad:

2 cups	fresh green beans	500 mL
2	ripe tomatoes	2
3	white Belgian endives	3

Vinaigrette:

¼ cup	balsamic vinegar	50 mL
1 tsp	Dijon mustard	5 mL
½ tsp	dried tarragon	2 mL
¾ cup	olive oil	175 mL
	Salt and pepper	

Goat Cheese Toast:

12	½-inch (1-cm) slices of French bread	12
¼ cup	olive oil	50 mL
½ lb	goat cheese	250 g

Trim ends from beans and place in saucepan, cover with water and ¼ tsp (1 mL) of salt and cook until tender crisp. Drain and plunge into cold water to stop the cooking and set the color. Drain and set aside in a large bowl. Remove center top from tomatoes and cut into wedges. Place in bowl. Quarter the endives, remove and discard center core and slice leaves on the diagonal. Add to beans and tomatoes, and toss well with vinaigrette.

Vinaigrette: In a small bowl, whisk together vinegar, Dijon mustard and tarragon. Add oil and continue whisking until emulsified. Season with salt and pepper. (For an interesting variation, substitute 2 tbsp or 25 mL of maple syrup for the Dijon mustard.)

Goat cheese toast: Preheat broiler. Brush bread slices with olive oil and broil briefly until golden and crisp (do not burn). Remove from broiler and spread with goat cheese and return to broiler for a minute to soften cheese, and then remove.

Place salad on individual plates and top with two slices of goat cheese toast.

Makes 6 servings.

SPINACH SALAD WITH MAPLE DRESSING

Spinach makes wonderful salad, especially complemented with this tangy maple dressing. If you can't select from a basket of loose leaves, look for a package that feels fresh and springs back from a gentle squeeze. Take the time to wash the spinach well and trim off any split, yellowing stems. This crunchy, filling salad is perfect as the main course of a light luncheon. Serve it with a crusty bread and soft white wine or sparkling, non-alcoholic apple cider.

8 oz	spinach	250 g
2	strips of bacon, cooked until crisp, and chopped	2
1	apple, unpeeled and diced	1
¼ cup	cheddar cheese, grated	50 mL
¼ cup	mozzarella cheese, grated	50 mL
	Maple Dressing:	
¾ cup	mayonnaise	175 mL
1 tbsp	lemon juice	15 mL
1 tsp	vinegar	5 mL
¾ cup	granulated sugar	175 mL
3 tbsp	pure maple syrup	45 mL
½ tsp	freshly chopped parsley	2 mL

Maple Dressing: Combine all of the dressing ingredients and blend until smooth. Store covered in the refrigerator. Yields 1¼ cups (300 mL).

Trim, wash and dry spinach and tear into bite-sized pieces. Place in a salad bowl and set aside.

Just before serving, pour desired amount of dressing over spinach and toss well to coat. Add bacon, apple and cheeses, toss lightly.

Makes 6 to 8 servings.

SCALLOPS WITH LIME TARRAGON VINAIGRETTE AND VEGETABLE SALAD

In Central and South America raw shellfish, marinated in lime juice (Seviche), is a popular dish. Uncooked scallops may be an acquired taste for many, however. This salad calls for cooked scallops, which are then tossed with a lime vinaigrette, making a salad that is reminiscent of its Spanish cousin.

Vegetable Salad Vinaigrette:

½ cup	olive oil	125 mL
1 tbsp	white vinegar	15 mL
1 tsp	dried oregano	5 mL
	Salt and pepper	

Vegetable Salad:

1	small carrot, cut into matchsticks	1
1	stalk celery, cut into matchsticks	1
4-6	mushrooms, quartered	4-6
½	small onion, peeled and sliced	½
1	cauliflower, florets only	1

Lime Tarragon Vinaigrette:

½ cup	lime juice	125 mL
¾ tsp	lime zest	3 mL
¾ tsp	shallots, chopped fine	3 mL
1½ tsp	fresh tarragon, chopped	7 mL
½ tsp	honey	2 mL
½ cup	olive oil	125 mL
	Salt and pepper	

Scallops:

1 lb	scallops	500 g
1	head of green or red leaf lettuce	1
	Fresh tarragon to garnish	

Vegetable Salad Vinaigrette: In a small bowl, combine oil, vinegar, oregano and salt and pepper, whisk until well blended.

Vegetable Salad: Blanch or steam vegetables (excluding mushrooms) for 2 to 3 minutes. Remove from heat, drain, add mushrooms and marinate for at least 6 to 8 hours in vegetable salad vinaigrette.

Lime Tarragon Vinaigrette: Combine and whisk together all ingredients for lime tarragon vinaigrette. Set aside.

Sauté scallops lightly. Place on bed of lettuce and sprinkle with lime tarragon vinaigrette; garnish with fresh tarragon. Surround scallops with vegetable salad and serve.

Makes 6 servings.

CRUNCHY POTATO SALAD

Potato salad is found in most collections of recipes. Here is one with a few new twists. It is a good dish to serve with boiled lobster. The green pepper, green onions and radishes add zip and crunch.

3 cups	white potatoes, peeled, cooked and cubed	750 mL
3	hardboiled eggs, peeled and chopped	3
1	large green pepper, seeded and chopped	1
½ cup	green onions, sliced	125 mL
6–8	radishes, thinly sliced	6–8
½ cup	unsalted peanuts	125 mL

Dressing:

½ cup	sour cream	125 mL
¼ cup	mayonnaise	50 mL
¼ cup	sweet pickle relish, drained	50 mL
1 tsp	Dijon mustard	5 mL
	Salt and freshly ground pepper	

In a large bowl, mix together cubed cooked potatoes, eggs and green pepper, onion and radish. Prepare dressing in a small bowl by blending sour cream, mayonnaise, relish and mustard until smooth and creamy; season to taste with salt and pepper. Combine dressing with potato mixture, stirring to coat potatoes. Cover and chill 2 to 4 hours before serving. Garnish with pepper rings, whole radishes and chopped unsalted peanuts.

Makes 6 servings.

CAESAR ATLANTIC

Visitors to Nova Scotia often have one thing on their dining agenda – seafood.
This salad, really a full meal, features a variety of shellfish and takes
the ubiquitous Caesar salad to seafood heaven.

Croutons:

¼ cup	olive oil	50 mL
3	cloves garlic, peeled and minced	3
1½ cups	French bread, cut into cubes	375 mL

Salad:

¼ lb	butter	125 g
3	cloves garlic, peeled and diced	3
16	shrimp, peeled and deveined	16
½ lb	medium-sized scallops	250 g
¾ lb	mussels	350 g
¼-½ lb	lobster meat	125-250 g
¼ cup	dry white wine	50 mL
2	eggs	2
½ cup	olive oil	125 mL
	Juice of ½ a lemon	
2	heads Romaine lettuce	2
6	anchovy fillets, minced (optional)	6
⅔ cup	freshly grated Parmesan cheese	150 mL
	Salt and pepper	

To make the croutons: In a heavy skillet, heat ¼ cup (50 mL) of olive oil. When the oil is hot but not smoky, add the minced garlic and brown slightly. Add the bread cubes and sauté, stirring often until browned. Remove from skillet with slotted spoon and place on a paper towel to drain.

To prepare the seafood for the salad: Melt the butter in a skillet over medium heat. Add the diced garlic and brown slightly. Add the shrimp, scallops, mussels and lobster meat and sauté for approximately 3 minutes or until the mussels begin to open. Stir in the white wine and continue cooking until the mussels are fully opened. Discard any mussels that do not open all the way. Remove seafood from the heat.

To prepare the salad: Begin by bringing a small saucepan of water to a boil and cook the eggs in their shells for 1 minute and remove from heat. In a small bowl, combine soft-boiled eggs, olive oil and lemon juice; blend until creamy. Break the Romaine lettuce into leaves and wash thoroughly, then dry in a salad spinner or pat dry with a tea towel. Break the lettuce into bite-sized pieces and place in a large salad bowl. Pour egg mixture over the salad and toss until lettuce is well coated. Add the minced anchovy, grated Parmesan cheese, croutons and salt and freshly ground pepper to taste, lightly tossing to blend ingredients. Place salad on four large dinner plates. With a slotted spoon, remove fish from cooking liquid,* place all the seafood except the mussels over each salad. Arrange the mussels around the outside of the salad.

The cooking liquid is excellent for use in soups, chowders and stock. Refrigerate or freeze for future use.

**Makes 4 large entrée servings
or
8 to 10 appetizer-sized servings.**

LAMB SALAD ON MIXED GREENS

Lamb is an unusual and wonderful ingredient for a salad. Use this one for a luncheon entrée or a buffet dish. Leftover leg of lamb that is rare to medium would be fine to use. As an alternative, cut some from a fresh leg that you are planning to roast and freeze it for later use.

1 lb	lamb, cut from leg	500 g
¼ cup	vegetable or walnut oil	50 mL
1 tsp	salt	5 mL
2 tbsp	green or black peppercorns	25 mL
2 cups	snow peas	500 mL
¼ tsp	freshly ground black pepper	1 mL
¼ tsp	ground rosemary	1 mL
¼ cup	orange juice, freshly squeezed	50 mL
1 cup	mandarin orange slices	250 mL
1	large apple, unpeeled, cored and diced	1
¼ cup	walnuts, chopped	50 mL
2 tbsp	raisins	25 mL
6 cups	salad greens, mixed	1.5 L

Slice the lamb into 1-inch (2.5-cm) thin strips. In a skillet or wok over medium heat, add oil and salt. Add lamb to heated oil and stir-fry for 2 to 3 minutes. Add peppercorns, snow peas, pepper, rosemary and orange juice; continue to stir-fry an additional 2 minutes. In a small bowl, combine mandarin orange slices, apple slices, walnuts and raisins; mix well. Stir fruit mixture into lamb and heat throughout. Serve on a bed of rinsed salad greens.

Makes 6 servings.

Meat and Poultry

Halifax
Dartmouth

HALIFAX AND DARTMOUTH

HALIFAX AND DARTMOUTH SIT ON EITHER SIDE OF THE SECOND-LARGEST NATURAL harbor in the world. The strategic location of the deep, ice-free harbor was not lost on the Canadian Navy, which historically has been headquartered here, protecting the east coast of North America.

A drive across one of the bridges linking the cities takes you over waters crowded with destroyers and frigates, the commuter ferries that have crossed the harbor since 1752, million-dollar yachts from around the world, supertankers, oil rigs ready for duty in the North Atlantic and tugboats keeping everything in chaotic order.

During World Wars I and II, tens of thousands of soldiers and sailors called Halifax home while their convoys fitted up and prepared for the treacherous trip to Europe. Many of the pubs that those men and women frequented are still open today, and the same live Maritime, Scottish and Irish music can still be enjoyed.

Pier 21 at the west side of the harbor was the first debarkation point in North America for an astonishing 1.5 million immigrants. To be sure, most people traveled on from Halifax, but those who stayed helped to give the city a multicultural atmosphere. For thousands of visitors, a trip to Halifax is a reconnection to personal and family history.

Halifax and Dartmouth are proud of their heritage. Many of the buildings dating back to 1700s have been restored as shops, residences and offices. Warehouses built by privateers who raided American ships (during the years when that type of behavior was acceptable) are now part of an innovative waterfront restoration.

The Citadel Hill dominates Halifax. The fortress at the top of the hill has done its duty for more than 250 years. No enemy ship has ever entered the harbor, but it has not been free from the devastation of war. In 1917, in the last days of World War I, the Belgian relief ship *Imo* collided with the French munitions ship *Mont Blanc*, setting off the most powerful man-made explosion before the atomic age, rattling windows 100 miles away and causing tremendous death and destruction. Among the first to respond were doctors and relief convoys from Boston. To this day, Nova Scotia sends a huge Christmas tree to the city of Boston in gratitude.

Many a tourist has been startled by the boom of the noon cannon, fired daily by the soldiers garrisoned behind the walls of the Citadel. At the bottom of the hill sits the town clock, presented to Halifax by Queen Victoria's father, Prince Edward. It hasn't missed a tick in 190 years.

At the south end of the Halifax peninsula is the 186-acre Point Pleasant Park, a natural area of woods, trails and beaches, bikes, dogs and people (and no cars). The park is owned by the British Crown and is the last outpost of the British Empire on North American soil. The park is rented to the people of Halifax for one shilling a year, paid in a ceremony in the park each spring. There are 749 years left on the 999-year lease, so you can't blame Haligonians for mistaking the parkland as their own.

In 1799, the Nova Scotia Legislature determined that "it would greatly tend to the benefit both of the town and the country if a . . . Market House were erected in Halifax for the sole use of persons bringing in from the country meat, poultry, butter and other victuals and in which they might expose such articles for sale." This formalized the status of the farmers' market, then celebrating its 50th birthday.

Charles Dickens visited the Halifax Farmers' Market in 1849. He found it to be "abundantly supplied and exceedingly cheap." At the time of the visit the market was the bustling, colorful center of retail life in the port cities of Halifax and Dartmouth. There are more shopping options these days, but for variety of foods and crafts and a place for buyers and sellers to socialize, the market can't be beaten.

"My grandmother began selling at the market in 1895," Mary Ann LaPierre told us, while we visited with her in her familiar spot behind one of the market tables. "She loaded her wagon with eggs, butter, beans, peas, beets, wild berries and wildflowers and at midnight loaded it onto the harbor ferry for the trip from Dartmouth to Halifax." Grandmother Catherine LaPierre retired in 1934 at the age of eighty-five and Mary Ann's father, Rufus, took over, building a greenhouse so that he could sell a wider variety of goods. Joyce, her mother, sold needlework and hand-knit socks and mittens alongside the produce.

Mary Ann still farms the homestead first settled by her grandmother, but life is easier now. She doesn't need the midnight ferry. She doesn't have to get up until 3:30 a.m. to load the truck and head for the market.

Market Day has not changed much in the past 250 years. The aisles are narrow and crowded, the tables overflow with all manner of fruits, vegetables, fresh and smoked meats and fowl, cheese, butter and cream, as well as practical crafts. The farmers and their customers really enjoy the whole process of buying and selling. The regulars see the product mix change as the seasons progress, and each week the chefs and home cooks create innovative menus on the spot, after surveying the ripe products available to them. Seasonal cooking is born at the market.

MARITIME PORK CASSOULET WITH CRANBERRIES AND PORT

Bistro-style food is not unique to France. The Nova Scotian dishes made with salt cod, mussels, potatoes, fresh greens and so on are very similar to their French counterparts. Cassoulet is a slow-baked stew of beans and meat. Pork is used in this version. The tang of the cranberries complements the pork, and the slow cooking in the port blends the flavors thoroughly. This dish is excellent when served with Blueberry Johnny Cake (page 125) and Chow Chow (page 143).

2 lb	pork, well trimmed, cut into 1-inch (2.5-cm) cubes	1 kg
1 tbsp	vegetable oil	15 mL
1½ cups	port	375 mL
2 cups	yellow-eyed or northern beans	500 mL
6 cups	water	1.5 L
1	medium onion, peeled and chopped	1
2	bacon slices, rolled and tied with string	2
3 tbsp	brown sugar	45 mL
3 tbsp	molasses	45 mL
3 tbsp	tomato purée	45 mL
¼ cup	orange juice, freshly squeezed	50 mL
½ tsp	orange zest	2 mL
1 tbsp	Dijon mustard	15 mL
1 tsp	ginger	5 mL
¾ tsp	ground white pepper	4 mL
1½ cups	cranberries, fresh or frozen	375 mL

In a large skillet, heat oil and brown the pork cubes on all sides. Pour off excess oil, add the port to the hot skillet, scraping up the browned bits (this is called deglazing) and remove from heat. Cool and refrigerate.

Add beans to water in a dutch oven large enough to hold all the ingredients. Bring to a boil and boil for 3 minutes. Remove from heat, let stand covered for 1 hour, then add remaining ingredients, except cranberries. Bake, covered, in a preheated oven at 350°F (180°C) for 1 hour. Add pork and port and continue to bake for an additional 1½ to 2 hours, checking every half-hour for doneness. If more liquid is required, add to keep the beans from drying out. Add cranberries during final 30 minutes of baking. Remove tied bacon slices before serving.

Makes 6 servings.

MEDALLIONS OF PORK WITH NOVA SCOTIA SCALLOPS AND BLUEBERRIES

Lean boneless pork medallions and sweet scallops make a good team.
Fruit sauce is not often used with seafood, but we think you will be pleasantly
surprised by this combination.

1 tsp	shallots, chopped	5 mL
1 tsp	butter	5 mL
½ cup	blueberries, mashed	125 mL
dash	sugar	dash
1 cup	beer (try a Nova Scotia brand)	250 mL
1 cup	pork or chicken stock, thickened with 1 tbsp (15 mL) cornstarch	250 mL
	Salt and pepper	
⅓ cup	whipping cream	75 mL
2 tbsp	butter	25 mL
2 lbs	pork tenderloin	1 kg
24	scallops	24

In a large skillet, sauté shallots in butter until translucent. Add mashed blueberries and sugar and bring to a boil. Stir in beer and cook for 2 to 3 minutes. Add pork or chicken stock and continue to cook for several more minutes. Season to taste with salt and pepper and gradually blend in cream.

Cut pork tenderloins into medallions approximately 1 inch (2.5 cm) thick and pound between sheets of wax paper until they are ½ inch (1 cm) thick.

Sauté pork medallions in butter 5 minutes; add scallops and continue to sauté an additional 5 minutes.

On warmed dinner plates, pour blueberry sauce, then top with sautéed scallops and pork.

Makes 8 servings.

ACADIAN TOURTIÈRE

*Meat-filled pies (savories) are found in many culinary cultures,
including the French Acadian. Their version is fragrant with spices and the sweetness
of oranges. You could make an extra pie or two and freeze them for later use.*

*Tourtière is the French name for the ceramic pie dish in which tourtes (pies) are
baked. It was adapted by the Acadians as the name of the finished pie.*

1 lb	lean ground beef	500 g
1 lb	lean ground pork	500 g
1	medium onion, peeled and diced	1
2	cloves garlic, finely diced	2
1 tsp each	ground cloves, cinnamon, allspice, nutmeg	5 mL each
1 tsp each	salt and freshly ground pepper	5 mL each
1	orange (both zest and juice)	1
2-3	slices white bread with crusts trimmed and cut into ½-inch (1-cm) cubes	2-3
¾ cup	beef stock	175 mL
	Pastry for double pie crust	
1	egg, slightly beaten	1

In a heavy saucepan with cover, combine beef, pork, onion, seasonings, orange juice and orange zest. Over medium heat, cook until meat is browned, stirring often and breaking meat into small pieces. Add bread cubes and mix until well blended. Remove from heat and allow to rest for 5 minutes. Next add beef stock, and if mixture appears to be runny, add additional bread cubes. Spoon meat mixture into two 6-in (15-cm) pastry-lined pie plates. Brush half of the beaten egg over the edges of the bottom crusts. Place the second crust on top and crimp with a fork. Bake at 400°F (200°C) for 30 to 35 minutes or until crust is golden brown, checking frequently.

Pie Crust:

1 cup	all-purpose flour	250 mL
½ tsp	salt	2 mL
½ cup	shortening	125 mL
	Cold water	

In a mixing bowl, combine flour and salt, cut in shortening (should be at room temperature) with a pastry blender to form a coarse crumb. Add just enough cold water to form a soft dough, taking care not to overmix. Chill for 30 minutes. Divide dough in half, place on a floured surface and roll out to desired size.

Makes one double pie crust.

BEEF ROULADE

A roulade is a meat fillet rolled around well-spiced minced meat or sausage and then cooked. The savory stuffing of sausage and spinach in this dish is an unusual and delicious way to cook a beef fillet. Not much beef is needed, since the finished dish is quite filling.

1–1½ lb	round steak	500–750 g
1 tsp	salt	5 mL
½ tsp	white pepper	2 mL
1 tsp	summer savory	5 mL
2 tbsp	prepared dill mustard	25 mL
3	hot Italian sausage links	3
¼ cup	all-purpose flour	50 mL
2 tbsp	butter	25 mL
1½ cup	dry red wine	375 mL
2 tbsp	tomato paste	25 mL

Prepare the meat by pounding the steak until approximately ¼ inch (0.5 cm) in thickness, cut into six 3- x 4-inch (7- x 10-cm) pieces. Season with salt, pepper and summer savory. Cover each slice with 1 tsp (5 mL) of dill mustard. Remove the sausage meat from the casings and place approximately 2 tbsp (25 mL) on each slice. Roll the meat and tie at both ends with white string or wrap like a cabbage roll. Cover the roulade in flour. In a skillet over medium heat, melt the butter and brown each roulade. In a heavy casserole dish, stir the red wine and tomato paste together until well blended. Add the roulades and bake, covered, in a preheated 325°F (160°C) oven for 1¼ hours. Check occasionally to ensure that there is sufficient liquid, adding more wine if required.

Remove roulades and place on a warmed serving platter. Pour cooking liquid over them before serving.

Makes 6 servings.

GARDEN-FRESH BEEF STEW WITH MAPLE DUMPLINGS

In this satisfying and filling stew, the flavors of rum and maple accent the beef and vegetables with a smooth sweetness.

1½ tsp	salt	7 mL
½ tsp	cayenne pepper	2 mL
1 tsp	freshly ground black pepper	5 mL
2 tbsp	all-purpose flour	25 mL
1½ lb	lean stewing beef, cut in chunks	750 g
2 tbsp	vegetable oil	25 mL
1	clove garlic, minced	1
2	bay leaves	2
¼ cup	dark rum	50 mL
4	potatoes, peeled and cut in chunks	4
4	carrots, peeled and cut in chunks	4
1	small turnip, peeled and cut in chunks	1
2	parsnips, peeled and cut in chunks	2
2	onions, coarsely chopped	2
1	small green pepper, cut in strips	1

Dumplings:

2 cups	all-purpose flour	500 mL
4 tsp	baking powder	20 mL
½ tsp	salt	2 mL
2 tbsp	shortening	25 mL
⅔ cup	milk	150 mL
⅓ cup	maple syrup	75 mL

In a small bowl, combine salt, peppers and flour. Place flour mixture in a plastic bag, drop in pieces of beef and shake well to coat. In a dutch oven, heat oil, and brown beef on all sides. Add sufficient water to cover and bring to a boil. Reduce heat and add garlic, bay leaves and rum and simmer for about 2 hours or until beef is almost tender. Add potatoes, carrots, turnip, parsnips, onions and green pepper and continue to simmer until vegetables are tender crisp.

Maple Dumplings: In a mixing bowl, combine flour, baking powder and salt, then cut in shortening. Combine milk and maple syrup in a small bowl and gradually add to flour mixture, mixing with a fork until batter is moist. Drop by spoonful onto top of beef stew. Cover pot and simmer for 15 to 20 minutes, until dumplings are cooked through.

Makes 6 to 8 servings.

SHEPHERD'S PIE

This is not the cafeteria food many of us think of as Shepherd's Pie. This dish is sophisticated in taste and easy to make and is the essence of comfort food. It keeps in the oven, stretches to feed unexpected guests and makes a good leftover.

6	large potatoes, peeled and cut into 2-in (5-cm) pieces	6
2 tbsp	butter	25 mL
½ cup	milk	125 mL
1 lb	ground lamb	500 g
1 lb	medium ground beef	500 g
2 tbsp	vegetable oil	25 mL
2	cloves garlic, peeled and minced	2
1	large onion, peeled and chopped	1
2	medium carrots, peeled and chopped	2
2 tbsp	all-purpose flour	25 mL
1 cup	red wine or beef stock	250 mL
1-14 oz tin	plum tomatoes	1-398 mL
1 tsp	dried thyme	5 mL
1 tsp	dried marjoram	5 mL
½ tsp	ground cumin	2 mL
⅓ tsp	English-style dry mustard	2 mL
	Salt and pepper	
2 tbsp	butter	25 mL

Place potatoes in a saucepan with ½ tsp (2 mL) salt and sufficient water to cover them. Bring to a boil, reduce heat and cook until potatoes are tender, approximately 30 minutes. Drain the potatoes, add butter and milk and mash until smooth. Set aside.

In a large skillet over medium heat, brown the ground lamb and beef, stirring occasionally to cook evenly. Drain and discard fat. Set meat aside in a large bowl.

Return the skillet to a medium heat; add oil, garlic, onion, carrots and flour. Cook for three minutes, stirring occasionally. Add the beef stock or wine, tomatoes, thyme, marjoram, cumin and mustard. Continue to cook for 10 minutes at a slow boil, stirring frequently. Add tomato mixture to cooked ground meats, stirring well to combine. Salt and pepper to taste. Place the mixture in a 9- x 12-inch (22- x 30-cm) metal or glass baking pan. Spoon the mashed potatoes over meat, covering the entire pan and taking care to seal the edges. Dot the potatoes with the butter and bake in a preheated 350°F (180°C) oven for 40 minutes or until potatoes become crusty and begin to brown.

Makes 6 to 8 servings.

LAMB CRANBERRY STEW

*Sweet lamb, tart berries and buttery vegetables are a grand combination,
easy and economical for crisp fall evenings.*

¼ cup	vegetable oil	50 mL
2 lb	boneless lamb shoulder, cubed	1 kg
2 tsp	salt	10 mL
¼ tsp	crushed thyme leaves	1 mL
4	whole cloves	4
1 tbsp	lemon juice, freshly squeezed	15 mL
1	clove garlic, diced	1
1 cup	beef stock	250 mL
1	medium onion, peeled and diced	1
1 cup	water	250 mL
5	medium carrots, peeled and quartered	5
6	medium potatoes, peeled and chunked	6
1 cup	cranberry sauce (whole berry–style, see page 52)	250 mL
2 tbsp	cornstarch	25 mL
¼ cup	water	50 mL

In a dutch oven or large saucepan, heat the oil and brown the lamb on all sides. Add salt, thyme, cloves, lemon juice, garlic, beef stock, onion and water. Cover and heat to boiling. Reduce heat and simmer for 45 minutes. Add carrots, potatoes and cranberry sauce, and more water, if necessary. Cover and simmer for 35 to 45 minutes or until lamb and carrots are tender. Dissolve cornstarch in water, add to stew and stir until thickened.

Makes 6 servings.

LAMB WITH FETA

Cape Breton Island and the Northumberland Shore both produce lamb of incomparable flavor. Some credit the climate, the area's sweet grass and the salt spray from the Gulf of St. Lawrence. We think that the human touch has a lot to do with it, coming from the generations of shepherds from the Highlands of Scotland, whose skill accompanied their descendants in the move to Nova Scotia from Scotland two hundred years ago.

In this "dressy" lamb dish, the tang of the feta cheese beautifully accents the sweet lamb. It is well worth a search for fresh oregano, basil and thyme.

1	egg	1
¼ cup	feta cheese, drained	50 mL
2 tbsp	whipping cream	25 mL
1	clove garlic, minced	1
1 tsp	fresh thyme chopped	5 mL
	(½ tsp/2 mL dried)	
½ tsp	fresh basil chopped	2 mL
	(¼ tsp/1 mL dried)	
	Salt and pepper	
1	rack of lamb	1

Blend egg, feta, cream, garlic and seasonings together to create a paste. On the loin side or meaty side of the rack, make a slit approximately 1 inch (2.5 cm) in diameter, from one end to the other. Using a piping bag or a long-handled spoon, stuff the feta mixture into the loin. Season the outside of the rack with salt and pepper and bake in preheated oven 425°F (220°C) for approximately 15 to 20 minutes.

For serving, carefully slice between each chop to show feta stuffing.

Makes 4 servings.

LEG OF LAMB IN YOGURT MARINADE

This recipe is Eastern European in origin, brought here by the Armenians and the Greeks. Marinating lamb in yogurt is a terrific way to create a moist leg with a great sauce.

1	leg of lamb (about 6.5 lb/3 kg) de-boned and tied	1

Marinade:

2½ cups	plain yogurt	625 mL
1 cup	onion, peeled and finely chopped	250 mL
½ cup	fresh dill, chopped or 3 tbsp/45 mL dry	125 mL
½ cup	olive oil	125 mL
2 tsp	salt	10 mL
½ tsp	freshly ground pepper	2 mL

Place lamb in a large, sturdy plastic bag. In a medium bowl, mix together all the marinade ingredients and pour into the bag. Seal tightly and turn a few times to coat the lamb well. Leave at room temperature for 2 to 3 hours, squeezing and turning the bag occasionally to coat the meat evenly. Preheat oven to 500°F (260°C). Remove lamb from bag and place in a baking pan large enough to accommodate the meat and the marinade. Spoon the marinade over the lamb and bake for 30 minutes. Reduce the heat to 375°F (190°C), turn the meat and baste with the marinade. Cover the pan tightly with foil and bake an additional 1 hour.

Remove the meat to a heated platter. Spoon the fat from the pan and discard, serving the remaining pan juices as accompaniment to the meat.

Makes 8 to 10 servings.

DRUNKEN CHICKEN

It is surprising that rum, rather than Scotch whiskey, is the favorite alcoholic beverage in Nova Scotia. This is because of the great sea routes that were opened between the province and the Caribbean by the schooner captains of the eighteenth century. The pairing of rum and fresh fruit in this chicken dish is evocative of the flavors of the Islands.

6	boneless, skinless chicken breasts	6
3	fresh peaches, cut in wedges	3

Glaze:

1½ cup	pure maple syrup	375 mL
3 tbsp	lemon juice, freshly squeezed	45 mL
1 tsp	lemon rind	5 mL
3 tbsp	dark rum	45 mL
¼ cup	butter	50 mL

Pound each chicken breast between pieces of wax paper until ½-inch (1-cm) thick. Place 3 peach wedges on one side of chicken breast and roll, keeping peaches on the inside, and pinning breast together with a toothpick if necessary. Bake in a preheated oven at 325°F (160°C) for 10 minutes. While chicken is baking, prepare glaze.

In a small saucepan, combine maple syrup, lemon juice and rind, rum and butter, and stir until all ingredients are blended. Simmer until sauce thickens. Remove chicken breasts from oven and coat with glaze. Return to oven and cook an additional 10 minutes or until chicken is done. Take remaining glaze and drizzle over the breasts of chicken before serving.

Makes 6 servings.

CRANBERRY-GLAZED CHICKEN

This chicken comes out of the oven with a beautiful, glistening glaze and bright flavor. Try plain or garlic mashed potatoes as an accompaniment.

1	chicken (3 lb/1.5 kg), cut into pieces	1
3 tbsp	oil	45 mL
1½ cups	fresh cranberry sauce (see below) or 14-oz. (398-mL) can of whole cranberry sauce	375 mL
¼ cup	soy sauce	50 mL
2 tbsp	lemon juice	25 mL
1 tsp	ground ginger	5 mL
⅓ cup	brown sugar	75 mL
1 tsp	dry mustard	5 mL
1	garlic clove, minced	1

Wipe chicken with a damp cloth and pat dry. In a large skillet, heat oil and lightly brown chicken pieces on both sides for about 15 minutes. Transfer chicken to a baking dish. Combine remaining ingredients and pour over chicken. Bake in preheated 350°F (180°C) oven for 45 minutes or until chicken is tender.

Makes 4 to 5 servings.

Fresh Cranberry Sauce

1 cup	granulated sugar	250 mL
½ cup	water	125 mL
2 cups	fresh or frozen cranberries	500 mL

Combine sugar and water in saucepan. Bring to a boil and add cranberries. Cook cranberries in boiling syrup, without stirring, until skins pop, about 10 minutes.

Photo: Fiddlehead Soup,
Cranberry-Glazed Chicken,
Potatoes with Horseradish Butter

CORIANDER CHICKEN WITH LINGUINE

Fresh coriander, easily grown in the northern herb garden, is known as cilantro. Many cooks are familiar with the use of cilantro in Mexican cooking, for salsas and other dishes. Here we use its piquant flavor in a chicken and pasta dish.

1 tbsp	peanut or other vegetable oil	15 mL
¾ lb	boneless, skinless, chicken breasts, cut in strips	350 g
1½	cloves garlic, minced	1½
¼ oz	fresh coriander (cilantro),* stems and leaves, finely chopped	10 g
2	small tomatoes, diced	2
¼ tsp	crushed, dried chili pepper	1 mL
1½ tsp	paprika	7 mL
½ cup	tomato juice	125 mL
1 lb	fresh pasta (fettucini or linguine), cooked	500 g

In a large skillet over medium heat, sauté chicken strips, garlic and coriander in peanut oil. When chicken starts to brown, add tomatoes, chili, paprika and tomato juice. Continue cooking, reducing sauce slightly. Add cooked pasta and toss.

For a more attractive presentation, use ½ lb of egg pasta and ½ lb of spinach pasta.

* *Fresh coriander must be used. Ground coriander is the seed of the plant and has a completely different flavor.*

Makes 4 servings.

Photo: From mid-summer to late fall, the farmers' markets and roadside stands overflow with gorgeous fruits and vegetables.

GRILLED BREAST OF PHEASANT WITH APPLE BRANDY SAUCE

Pheasant is becoming more available in farmers' markets' as well as the larger supermarkets. It is a lovely, rich-tasting bird. The apple brandy sauce is sparkling and works well with chicken if pheasant can't be found.

4	breasts of pheasant or chicken, boneless and skinless	4
	Apple Brandy Sauce:	
1	onion, peeled and diced	1
2	cloves garlic, diced	2
2 cups	apple juice	500 mL
3 cups	whipping cream	750 mL
1 oz	brandy	25 mL
½ cup	apple, peeled and diced	125 mL
	Salt and pepper	
	Apple slices	

Cook the pheasant or chicken on a barbecue, electric grill or broiler, for approximately 5 minutes per side, being careful not to overcook.

Sauce: In a saucepan, combine onion, garlic and apple juice over medium heat; cook mixture until reduced by ¾ of original volume. Add whipping cream and continue to cook until mixture has further reduced by ½ of its volume. Strain mixture through a fine sieve to make a smooth velvety sauce. Add brandy and apple, and salt and pepper to taste. Serve hot over pheasant or chicken, and garnish with fresh apple slices.

Makes 4 servings.

RAPPIE PIE

Rappie Pie has been cooked in Nova Scotia kitchens since the 1600s. It is a simple one-dish meal that is not unlike a pot pie. The potatoes encase the chicken under a golden crust. Rappie Pie can be made around a wide variety of meat or seafood, although chicken is the most common.

1	chicken (3-4 lb/1.5-2 kg), cut up	1
6 cups	chicken stock	1.5 L
1 tsp	ground thyme	5 mL
½ tsp	ground bay leaves and poultry seasoning	2 mL
½ tsp	poultry seasoning	2 mL
2 tbsp	salt	25 mL
1 tbsp	pepper	15 mL
10 lb	potatoes, peeled and finely grated	4.5 kg
1	medium onion, chopped	1
8	strips of bacon, 2 of them finely chopped	8

Place cleaned chicken and seasonings in a large pot. Cover chicken with cold water and simmer for 1½ to 2 hours, or until meat falls away readily from the bones. Cool. Remove meat and cut into pieces. Return bones to pot and continue cooking for one hour.

Peel potatoes, soaking in cold water to retain color until needed. Grate potatoes finely with a hand grater or in food processor. Grate 10 potatoes at a time, placing each lot in a cloth bag and squeezing until all the water and starch are removed and the potatoes are quite dry. (Measure the liquid from the potatoes as an equal amount of stock will be added later.) To prevent discoloration, cover grated potatoes with a wet tea towel.

Loosen squeezed potatoes into a large pan and gradually add the hot stock in the amount equal to liquid removed from potatoes. Stir slowly to scald potatoes until they look jelly-like, making sure there are no lumps.

Cover the bottom of a well-greased 17- x 24- x 2-inch (45- x 60- x 5-cm) pan with half of the potatoes. Next, arrange pieces of chicken, chopped onion and 2 slices of finely chopped bacon over the potatoes. Cover with the remaining potatoes, arranging the remaining bacon strips on top.

Bake in a preheated 400°F (200°C) oven for 1½ to 2 hours or until crust forms on top. Serve immediately. As an option, chill overnight and the Rappie Pie will gel and thicken more. Cut into pieces and fry in butter until golden crust is formed on all sides. Serve with hot cranberry or apple sauce.

Makes 8 to 10 servings.

DUCK WITH GOLDEN APPLE RINGS

The problem with many duck recipes is that the resulting dish is either dry or greasy. This duck preparation, using a liquid cooking medium, produces a crisp-skinned, moist bird, with much of the fat removed.

1 5-lb	duck, cut into serving pieces (2 breasts, 2 whole legs, 2 wings)	1 2.2-kg
1 tbsp	vegetable oil	15 mL
1	medium onion, peeled and chopped	1
2	garlic cloves, minced	2
½ tsp	dried marjoram	2 mL
½ tsp	sweet paprika	2 mL
1¼ cups	chicken stock	300 mL
½ cup	port	125 mL
2	medium carrots, peeled and diced	2
1 tsp	cornstarch (dissolve in 1 tbsp/15 mL of cold water)	5 mL
	Juice of 1 orange	1
3 tbsp	butter	50 mL
4	apples, peeled, cored, sliced into ½-inch (1-cm) thick rings and drizzled with juice of 1 lemon	4
	Salt and pepper	

Trim as much fat from duck as possible and prick the skin all over with a sharp knife. Dry the duck with a towel and season with salt and pepper. In a heavy-bottomed dutch oven or casserole dish, heat the oil over medium heat and brown the duck, a few pieces at a time, setting them aside as they are browned. Pour off all but ½ tbsp (7 mL) of the fat and add the onion, cooking it until it is translucent. Add the garlic, marjoram and paprika and cook for 1 minute, stirring constantly. Add the stock and port and bring to a boil. Place the duck pieces, skin side up, in the dutch oven in one layer and cover. Place on the middle shelf of a preheated 350°F (180°C) oven and bake for 45 minutes. Add the carrots and continue braising for another 10 minutes or until duck and carrots are tender. Remove the carrots, set aside, keeping warm. Remove the duck and place on a broiler pan. Skim the fat from braising liquid and place liquid over medium heat on the stove, bringing to a boil. Add cornstarch and the orange juice and reduce to a simmer for 1 minute. Remove from heat, check seasonings and cover to keep warm.

Melt the butter in a large frying pan. When the butter is hot, add the apple rings in a single layer and cook over medium heat until golden brown on one side; flip and brown the other side. Remove from heat. Preheat broiler and broil duck pieces until skin is crisp (approximately 2 minutes).

To serve, set a piece of duck on a heated plate. Place some carrots around and spoon sauce over the top. Place three or four apple rings on the duck and off to the side.

Makes 4 servings.

TURKEY FILLETS WITH APPLE RUM SAUCE

Boneless turkey parts are an increasingly popular way of using this low-fat bird. The sauce for this dish does not call for any butter or cream, but the honey and rum create a rich-tasting gravy without the fat.

4	turkey fillets	4
½ cup	apple juice	125 mL
1 tbsp	dark rum	15 mL
	Salt and pepper to taste	

	Apple Rum Sauce:	
⅔ cup	apple juice	175 mL
2 tbsp	dark rum	25 mL
2 tsp	honey	10 mL
1 tbsp	cornstarch	15 mL
2 tbsp	cold water	25 mL

Combine ½ cup (125 mL) apple juice, 1 tbsp (15 mL) rum and salt and pepper for marinade. In a shallow dish, pour marinade over turkey, cover and marinate for 2 hours in the refrigerator. Grill turkey fillets on a barbecue or electric grill or broil them in the oven, until pinkness disappears, about 5 minutes on each side.

Apple Rum Sauce: In a saucepan, combine apple juice, rum and honey and bring to a boil over medium heat. Stir cornstarch into cold water and add to boiling liquid, stirring continuously until well blended. Cook for 1 minute.

To serve, drizzle apple rum sauce over each turkey fillet. Garnish with fresh apple wedges.

Makes 4 servings.

Fish

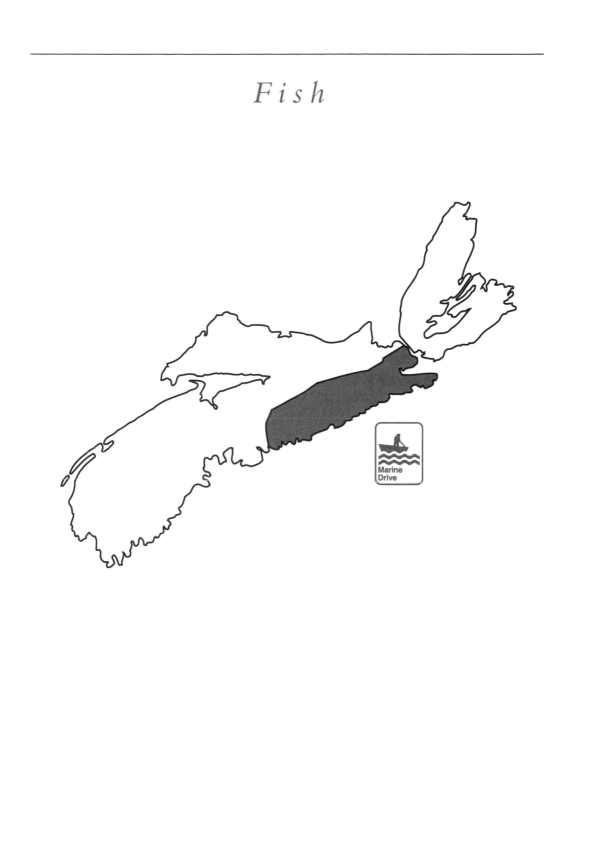

Marine
Drive

MARINE DRIVE

IN A PROVINCE WITH 4,625 MILES (7450 KM) OF COASTLINE AND UNDER 900,000 residents, Nova Scotia could hardly be considered crowded. For those who still feel the need for solitude, the Marine Drive, along Nova Scotia's Eastern Shore, is the answer. The shore road begins at the Strait of Canso, which separates mainland Nova Scotia from Cape Breton Island, and ends at the outskirts of Halifax and Dartmouth. Along the way it wanders more than 250 miles (400 km), clinging to the shoreline and passing by the most uninhabited and undeveloped area of the province. Here are the beaches where you will not run into another soul – only crashing surf in front of you and wild cranberry barrens and wildlife behind you. On a recent drive near a beach, we rounded a curve in the road and spotted an odd bird perched on a telephone pole. It looked like a bald eagle but had a strangely curved beak. Looking closer, what appeared to be the beak was, in fact, a freshly caught fish on its way to the eagle's nest.

The villages, with names like Ecum Secum, Necum Teuch, Mushaboom, Chezzetcook and West Newdy Quoddy, beg to be explored. These places, most with fewer than 200 residents living along the seabound coast, demonstrate appreciation for family lineage, hard work and delight in nature's gifts.

The weather along the Eastern Shore is soft in the summer, but fiercely dramatic in the winter. Fog often shrouds the coastline. A tourism official once suggested that Nova Scotia create a marketing campaign promoting its foggy weather, convinced that it would appeal to the tourists. There was considerable sputtering from those who preferred to sell the province as a place where wind, rain, ice and fog are so unusual they are hardly worth noting. But there is an appeal in the adventure of driving rain-slicked highways, feeling the salt spray from the waves overcoming the shoreline boulders and seeking the refuge of a steaming bowl of chowder alongside a blazing fire in a local inn.

The Marine Drive is separated from the more settled inland areas by deep forests, cut by rivers headed for open oceans. The rivers are known to sport fishermen for the finest salmon and trout fly-fishing available. There are salmon and trout pools here that have been fished for hundreds of years. The secret of their location rests with the registered guides who accompany the sport fishermen.

Over 100 years ago, there was the notion that the coastline would soon teem with activity. Gold was found near some of the rivers and the rush began. Villages sprang up, roads were cut into the woods and miners and would-be miners arrived in large numbers (large at least by Nova Scotia standards). As has often happened in the fickle mining business, the gold ran out and the mine sites became home to moose, deer, mink, muskrats, beaver and other forest animals.

The villages of the Eastern Shore are small and oriented to the sea. In some places, Sunday worshippers still arrive by boat to attend oceanside churches. While deep-sea fishing is still the main livelihood, sea farmers are now found along the many inlets and bays of the Eastern Shore. Their crops are culti-vated mussels and oysters, a relatively new industry with great growth potential. Cultivated shellfish are cleaner and more even in size and quality than the wild variety. The flavor is pure and sweet.

"Did you know that you can tell the age of a fish by its earbone? Just count the rings like you would a tree." That tidbit of fishing information was given to us by Randy Baker, whom we met in the small village of Head of Jeddore. (The consumer measures the age of a fish in hours from landing to the table; the fisherman measures the age of a fish from hatching to the net.) There are about 300 families in the area around the village; 100 of them are Bakers, whose Dutch/German ancestors, the Diefenbakers, arrived in 1756. "My whole family has fished for generations," Randy explained. "We are licensed for lobster and ground fish like herring, mackerel, cod, haddock, hake and cusk."

Lobster is where the real money is for the modern fisherman in Nova Scotia, but even that fishery is subject to wide fluctuations in the price offered at the dock by the large wholesalers who ship the catch to markets in Canada, Europe and, increasingly, to Japan. The heavily regulated lobster season along the Eastern Shore runs from April 20 to June 20. That's not an easy time to fish; the weather is very unpredictable and there is not much romance in a sunrise on the North Atlantic (the time the lobsterman needs to be at sea) when the raw wind is howling at 50 plus miles per hour (80 km/h) and the temperature is below zero Fahrenheit. The water is very cold, about 32°F (0°C), in April, "warming" to 42°F (6°C) in June. But there is an advantage to the timing of the Eastern Shore season. The cold water provides a better-quality lobster, plumper flesh filling the hard shell, with a minimum of empty space in the tail and the claws.

The lobsters begin molting in September and October when the water is at its warmest. Randy gave us a quick lecture on molting. "The shell softens and cracks along the top, then the lobster crawls out. Have you ever wondered why you don't see many lobster shells along the beach? Well, to speed up the hardening of the new shell, the lobster eats the old one to get the calcium." The lobster is very busy during molting time, since that is the only time it can mate. There is a window of 6 to 10 hours before the new shell hardens too much to allow mating. After that it takes 10 months for a baby lobster to hatch.

The lobster catch is celebrated around Nova Scotia. The map of the coastline was divided by the Department of Fisheries into districts to protect the lobster population. Fishing is permitted within each district during specific weeks or months known as a "season." Newspapers and bulletin boards almost always announce a lobster supper within driving distance. The feasts feature this king of shellfish, along with a variety of homemade chowders, rolls and desserts. The food is often prepared from heritage recipes, handed down for generations. Most dinners take place in church halls or the community centers, the centers of social life in small towns, and are the kind of informal gatherings where history comes alive. Attend a lobster supper in Head of Jeddore and the Bakers will surely be in evidence.

HOW TO COOK A LOBSTER

Lobster are at their best when prepared as simply as possible and served either hot or cold, shelled or in the shell, accompanied with melted butter, lemon wedges and lots of napkins. The traditional Nova Scotia way of cooking lobster is in a boiling pot of salt water directly from the ocean on a sandy beach over an open wood fire.

To prepare lobster at home, first ensure that the lobster is alive by checking for movement – pull its tail back to see if it springs back to the curled position. Place the live lobster headfirst into salted, boiling water; 1 tbsp (15 mL) salt per 1 quart (1 L) water. Cover the pot. Begin timing once water returns to a rolling boil and cook for 10 minutes for the first 1 lb (500 g) and 3 minutes for each additional 1 lb (500 g). The lobster is cooked when it is bright red and the legs pull away from the body with ease.

If by chance you have any lobster left over, it can be easily frozen.

Points for freezing:
Freeze lobster after it has been cooked and cooled.

For best results, freeze shelled lobster meat. Place meat in a freezer container and cover with a cold brine solution. Leave 1 inch (2.5 cm) space, seal tightly and label.

Whole cooked lobster can be frozen by placing it in a freezer container and covering it with a brine solution.

Freeze lobster at 0°F (18°C) or below. Lobster will keep for 4 to 6 months.

Brine solution: ¼ cup (50 mL) salt for each 1 quart (1 L) fresh water.

Note: If lobster meat is to be frozen for less than one month, a brine solution is not necessary.

LOBSTER SHANNON

This wonderful combination of lobster and pasta was developed as a dinner for two, since it's such an easy-to-make meal, perfect for a quiet evening with a special person. Of course it can be doubled, or more, for less intimate gatherings.

¼ cup	white wine	50 mL
1 tbsp	lemon juice, freshly squeezed	15 mL
3 grinds	black peppercorns	3 grinds
6 oz	cooked lobster meat	180 g
pinch	salt	pinch
½ cup	seafood velouté (see below)	125 mL
¼ cup	whipping cream	50 mL
6 oz	cooked fettucini or linguine	180 g

In a skillet over medium heat, mix together white wine, lemon juice, ground peppercorns and lobster, and salt. Quickly sauté until warmed, add hot velouté, whipping cream and cooked pasta. Simmer gently for 2 to 3 minutes. Adjust salt and freshly ground pepper to taste.

Seafood Velouté:

1½ tsp	butter	7 mL
1½ tsp	flour	7 mL
½ cup	fish stock	125 mL
pinch	nutmeg	pinch
	Salt and pepper	

Melt butter in top of double boiler. Stir in flour; when well blended, add fish stock and stir over low heat until blended and thickened. Strain through a fine sieve and season with nutmeg and salt and pepper to taste.

Makes 2 servings.

Sautéed Salmon with Walnut Honey Sauce

Fish and nuts are an unusual combination. The crunch adds a dimension of texture that is a little surprising. The spicy salmon and honey-sweetened sauce play off each other.

1¼ lb	salmon fillet	625 g
1 tbsp	salt	15 mL
1 tbsp	ground black pepper	15 mL
1 tbsp	garlic powder	15 mL
1½ tsp	cayenne pepper*	7 mL
⅓ cup	butter	75 mL
¼ cup	walnuts, coarsely chopped	50 mL
¼ cup	fish stock	50 mL
¼ cup	honey	50 mL
1 oz	fresh thyme	30 g

Cut salmon into 8 cubes, approximately 2½ oz (70 g) each. In a small bowl, combine salt, black pepper, garlic powder and cayenne pepper. Roll each salmon piece in the spice mixture. Blacken the salmon in an iron or heavy skillet that has been preheated on high for approximately 15 minutes or until it smokes; cook salmon approximately 5 minutes on each side. Remove from heat. In a saucepan over medium heat, melt the butter and sauté the walnuts for 2 to 3 minutes. Add the fish stock and the honey, and simmer for 5 to 6 minutes. Complete the sauce by adding the fresh thyme. Pour sauce onto 4 warmed dinner plates; top each with 2 pieces of the blackened salmon.

* The cayenne pepper may be reduced or increased to suit personal tastes – this particular spice mixture is hot.

Makes 4 servings.

POACHED SALMON WITH SWEET MUSCAT SAUCE

The fresh Atlantic salmon found in the fish market is more often than not farm-raised, ensuring uniform quality and freshness. Nova Scotia has many well-known salmon rivers, where a wild salmon can be a fisherman's reward (although the serenity of the place is a reward, even if a salmon is not caught).

Poaching is a delicious way of preparing a thick fillet. The poaching liquid is important and is another reason for keeping a flavorful fish stock in the freezer. Please do not overcook the fish, and remember that poaching is done in a barely simmering liquid for about 5 to 7 minutes (for a 6-oz/180 g fillet).

There are many wonderful sauces that work well on poached salmon, from the traditional Hollandaise to the garlicky, bright pesto. The unusual sauce featured in this recipe is made with a dessert wine such as muscat (now produced on the Northumberland Shore) and is quite delightful.

½ cup	sweet muscat wine or other dessert wine	125 mL
½ cup	fish stock	125 mL
½ cup	fresh-squeezed orange juice	125 mL
4	salmon fillets (6 oz/180 g each)	4
½ cup	whipping cream	125 mL
	Salt and pepper	

In a large skillet, add wine, fish stock and orange juice and bring to a boil. Lightly season the salmon with salt and pepper, then place in the skillet and cover, reducing heat to low. Simmer for approximately 5 to 7 minutes until done (salmon will be flaky). Remove salmon from the skillet and place on a heated platter.

Complete the sauce by reducing the cooking liquid to half of its original volume. Add the cream and reduce to half again; season with salt and pepper to taste. Pour sauce onto serving plate and top with salmon. Serve with fresh pasta or rice and fresh asparagus, peas or beans.

Makes 4 servings.

PLANKED SALMON WITH TARRAGON BUTTER

Here's a dish you're unlikely to see on many menus. Planking fish is a tradition that was begun by the Mi'kmaqs, the original residents of Nova Scotia. The whole fish was strapped to a thick wooden plank and set over an open fire until cooked through. The wood imparted a smoky flavor that enhanced the sweet salmon. We have adapted this recipe for the home kitchen. It is very easy to make, and this dish will be received with delight by all salmon lovers.

Tarragon Butter:

½ cup	butter, softened	125 mL
1	small clove garlic, minced	1
1 tsp	lemon juice	5 mL
1 tbsp	fresh tarragon, finely chopped or 1 tsp (5 mL) dry tarragon, soaked 30 minutes in 2 tbsp (25 mL) of warm water, drain excess water.	15 mL
½ tsp	grated lemon rind	2 mL

Fillets:

4	fillets of Atlantic Salmon (6 oz/180 g each)	4
1-2	untreated cedar shingles (available at lumber yards) Lemon twist Sprigs of fresh tarragon	1-2

Tarragon Butter: Combine butter, garlic, lemon juice, tarragon and lemon rind and mix well. Place on a sheet of plastic wrap, form into a log and wrap. Refrigerate butter roll for 4 hours or overnight.

Fillets: Prepare the cedar shingles by soaking them (depending on size, one shingle may hold the four fillets) in water for 1 hour. Remove shingle(s) from water and place salmon fillets skin side down. In a preheated 350°F (180°C) oven, set the shingle(s) on the middle rack and bake for 10 minutes or until salmon flakes easily.

Meanwhile, remove butter from refrigerator and slice into 8 rounds. Remove salmon from oven and carefully place each fillet on a plate, using a metal spatula. Place 1 or 2 rounds of butter on each fillet.

Garnish with lemon twist and sprigs of fresh tarragon.

Makes 4 servings.

Photo: Neil Harbour Swordfish with Three Pepper Sauce, Planked Salmon with Tarragon Butter

SMOKED SALMON PASTA

A marvellous recipe when you want an elegant dish that can be prepared in no time.
The smoked salmon can be kept frozen and quickly thawed for tossing with the pasta.

8 oz	dry fettucini	250 g
1 tbsp	vegetable oil	15 mL
2 tbsp	butter	25 mL
1	green pepper, diced	1
1	red pepper, diced	1
2	green onions, sliced in ½-inch (1-cm) pieces	2
½ cup	whipping cream	125 mL
12	fresh chive stems, chopped	12
2	tomatoes, peeled and diced	2
8 oz	smoked salmon, diced	250 g
	Salt and pepper	
	Tomato slices	
	Fresh basil leaves	

Cook pasta in 2 quarts (2 L) of boiling water with salt and oil until tender but still firm. In a large skillet over medium heat, melt the butter and sauté the green and red peppers and onions. Add the cream, chives, tomatoes and smoked salmon, season to taste with salt and pepper, stir until heated. Add drained pasta to smoked salmon and vegetables and sauté lightly; check seasonings.

Serve in a warmed deep plate and garnish with fresh tomato slices and fresh basil leaves.

Makes 4 servings.

Photo: Nova Scotia's coastal ports
harbor these colorful fishing boats
which travel thousands of miles a year
in search of their catch.

TROUT FILLET WITH FRESH SALMON

Here is a dinner-party dish that uses the unlikely combination of salmon and trout to produce a beautiful entrée. Boneless trout fillets should be available from the fish market. Steaming the fish maintains the fresh flavor.

White Wine Sauce:

½ cup	white wine	125 mL
1 tbsp	shallots, chopped	15 mL
⅓ cup	mushrooms, thinly sliced	75 mL
2 tbsp	white roux (see below)	25 mL
⅓ cup	fish stock	75 mL
¼ cup	whipping cream	50 mL

Stuffing:

8 oz	cooked salmon fillets	250 g
⅔ cup	fish stock	175 mL
2	egg whites	2
¼ cup	whipping cream	50 mL
2 tbsp	brandy	25 mL
dash	tabasco sauce	dash
	Salt and pepper	

Fillets:

4	boneless trout fillets	4

Sauce: In a saucepan, combine white wine, shallots and mushrooms and reduce to half the original volume. Add fish stock and whisk in white roux. Simmer for 5 minutes, and whisk in whipping cream; set aside.

Stuffing: In a saucepan over medium heat, poach salmon in the fish stock until salmon is flaky, approximately 10 minutes. Remove salmon, checking for bones, before placing in a food processor. Add the egg whites, whipping cream, brandy, tabasco sauce, and salt and pepper to taste. Quickly blend until salmon has broken into small pieces and ingredients are well combined.

Fillets: Spread the stuffing evenly on two of the fillets. Cover with the remaining fillets and cut each resulting "sandwich" in half. You will have four portions. Place each portion in a steamer basket over boiling water and steam until the trout flakes easily, approximately 8 to 10 minutes. Place stuffed trout on a warmed plate and cover with wine sauce. Garnish with sprigs of fresh dill or chives.

White Roux: In a small saucepan over medium heat, melt 1 tsp (5 mL) butter, add 1 tsp (5 mL) all-purpose flour, blend until smooth; add 4 tsp (20 mL) cream, stirring until well blended.

Makes 4 servings.

SEABASS WITH WHITE PEPPERCORN SAUCE

Either seabass or ocean perch works equally well for this recipe. The white peppercorns are spicy and make a bright sauce.

1 tbsp	white peppercorn	15 mL
4	seabass fillets (6 oz/180 g each)	4
2 tbsp	olive oil	25 mL
	Sauce:	
1 tsp	butter	5 mL
1 tbsp	shallots, chopped	15 mL
2 oz	brandy	50 mL
1 cup	fish stock	250 mL
½ cup	beef consommé or veal stock	125 mL
½ cup	whipping cream	125 mL
	Salt, to taste	

Put whole white peppercorn on a cutting board, and with the bottom of a skillet crush the pepper to a medium grain.

Make a few incisions on the skin side of the fish to keep it from curling while cooking. Salt the fish very lightly and sprinkle half of the mignonette on the flesh side of the fish. In a very hot sauté pan, heat the olive oil and place the fish skin up. Sauté until brown and then turn and sauté skin side until brown. Remove and keep warm.

Sauce: Discard any fat from the pan, melt the butter and add the shallots and remaining mignonette; sauté lightly. Then add the brandy and flambé. To flambé, allow brandy to heat slightly, and then ignite; be careful, as it flames high. Now add the fish and meat stock and reduce by half. Whisk in the cream, reduce by a third, add salt to taste.

Pour sauce on serving plates and top with seabass fillets.

Makes 4 servings.

FILLETS OF SOLE WITH LOBSTER FILLING

Sole is a mild white fish, which in this easy-to-make classic is complemented by the rich flavor of lobster stuffing. Accompany with a simple green vegetable and perhaps new potatoes cooked in their jackets and tossed with some butter and chives.

Stuffing:

¼ cup	butter	50 mL
½ cup	onions, finely chopped	125 mL
2 cups	fresh mushrooms, coarsely chopped	500 mL
6	whole wheat melba toast	6
	Salt and pepper	
½ cup	fresh chopped parsley	125 mL

Sauce:

¼ cup	butter	50 mL
¼ cup	all-purpose flour	50 mL
2 cups	light cream	500 mL
⅓ cup	white wine	75 mL
	Salt and pepper	

Fillets:

6	fresh sole fillets (8 oz/250 g each)	6
½ lb	cooked lobster meat, chopped	250 g

Stuffing: In a skillet over medium heat, melt the butter, add the onions and sauté until tender but not browned. Add the mushrooms and continue to sauté for one minute. Place melba toast in a food processor or a blender and blend to form coarse crumbs. Stir parsley and coarse melba toast crumbs into mushroom mixture. Mix well and season with salt and freshly ground pepper to taste.

Sauce: In a small saucepan, melt butter over medium heat and add the flour. Cook 2 to 3 minutes while stirring. Add light cream. Cook until smooth and thickened. Whisk in white wine. Continue to cook a few more minutes. Add salt and pepper.

Fillets: Rinse the sole and pat dry; generously season with salt and pepper. Spread each fillet with one-sixth of the stuffing mixture, top with one-sixth of lobster meat. Roll each fillet up; place seam side down in a buttered 8- x 10-inch (20- x 25-cm) pan. Pour sauce over the fish and cover loosely with foil.

Bake in a preheated 350°F (180°C) oven for 40 minutes, basting several times with the sauce and sliding the fish about to prevent sticking. Serve immediately.

Makes 6 servings.

HALIBUT WITH SAFFRON LEMON BUTTER

The secret of delicious fish is keeping it moist. One of the reasons for frying fish is to create a crust that holds in the natural juices. This recipe, which uses oriental rice paper in place of breading to seal in the juices without the added calories and fat of frying, also offers a unique way of presenting the finished dish.

2 tbsp	olive oil	25 mL
4	halibut fillets (5 oz/150 g each)	4
¾ cup	fresh wild mushrooms (shitake, chanterelles, oyster) or cultivated mushrooms, diced	175 mL
1	whole tomato, blanched, skinned, seeds removed and diced	1
1 tsp	dried basil	5 mL
4	sheets Thai rice paper (soaked for 1 minute in warm water before use) Salt and pepper	4

Saffron Lemon Butter Sauce:

1	lemon, sliced	1
1 tbsp	water	15 mL
1 cup	butter	250 mL
3-4	saffron threads	3-4

In a skillet over medium heat, place 1 tbsp (15 mL) of olive oil. Lightly sauté halibut fillets on both sides, remove from heat and cool.

In a small saucepan, add rest of olive oil and sauté the mushrooms, tomato and basil, season with salt and pepper and cool.

Soak the rice paper. Lay 4 sheets of soaked rice paper flat on table and place a quarter of the tomato, mushroom and basil mixture in center of each piece. Then place 1 halibut fillet on top of each. Fold in edges, turn over and place in a greased casserole or baking dish. Bake in a preheated oven at 375°F (190°C) for 15 to 20 minutes or until rice paper is crisp.

To make saffron butter sauce: Combine lemon slices and water in a medium saucepan over medium heat. Slowly stir in butter; heat but do not boil. Then add saffron. Remove lemon slices.

To serve, place a quarter of the lemon butter on each of 4 serving plates. Place halibut on top of butter. Serve with rice and vegetables.

Makes 4 servings.

SALT COD GRATIN

Salt cod was the staple of generations of Nova Scotians. Enough cod was caught and salted to last the entire winter. Despite the name, well-prepared salt cod is anything but salty and produces a delicate and delicious dish that cannot be duplicated with fresh fish.

This gratin is very much a Nova Scotia heritage recipe. (The word "gratin" does not necessarily mean a dish covered with cheese, but rather one that develops a thin crust when browned in an oven or under a broiler.)

1 lb	skinless, boneless, salt cod	500 g
2 cups	milk	500 mL
1	herb bouquet*	1
2 lb	baking potatoes, peeled and thinly sliced	1 kg
1	onion, peeled and thinly sliced	1
2	cloves garlic, minced	2
2	large egg yolks	2
½ cup	whipping cream	125 mL
	Salt and freshly ground pepper	
3 tbsp	unsalted butter	45 mL

The day prior to serving, place salt cod in a large bowl of cold water, cover and soak in the refrigerator, changing the water 3 or 4 times during the soaking period. The next day, drain and rinse the cod. Place the cod in a large saucepan, adding enough cold water to cover, and bring to the boiling point over medium heat. At this time remove the pan from the heat and allow to stand for 15 minutes. Drain and remove any bones or skin from the fish and break into bite-sized pieces.

In a large saucepan, combine the milk and herb bouquet and bring to a simmer over medium heat; remove from heat when milk starts to steam. Allow to stand for 15 minutes. Add the thinly sliced potatoes, onion and garlic, return to stove and cook over medium heat until the potatoes are tender (15 to 20 minutes). Remove the herb bouquet.

In a mixing bowl, combine the egg yolks and cream and whisk until smooth. Stir the egg mixture into the undrained, cooked potatoes. Season with salt and pepper to taste.

With 1 tsp (5 mL) of the butter, grease a gratin or other Pyrex-type baking dish. Place half of the potato mixture into the dish, add the cod and top with remaining potatoes. Dot the top with remaining butter and bake in a preheated 350°F (180°C) oven for 45 minutes or until the top is golden brown.

Makes 6 servings.

Herb Bouquet:

Tie together: 3 sprigs fresh parsley
1 sprig fresh thyme
1 bay leaf

or:

Place in a cheesecloth bag:
½ tsp/2 mL dried parsley
½ tsp/2 mL dried thyme
1 bay leaf

POACHED SOLE WITH TOMATO VINAIGRETTE

Sole, with its delicate flavor and snowy white color, works well with this sauce that carries the sweetness of the tomato and the tartness of the vinegar.

6	sole fillets (6 oz/180 g each)	6

Poaching Broth:

¼ cup	fish stock	50 mL
¼ cup	dry white wine	50 mL
1	bay leaf	1
pinch	dried thyme	pinch

Vinaigrette:

1 cup	olive oil	250 mL
⅓ cup	red wine vinegar	75 mL
½ cup	fresh tomato purée	125 mL
1½ tsp	salt	7 mL
½ tsp	black pepper	2 mL
1 tsp	granulated sugar	5 mL
2 tbsp	chopped fresh basil or ½ tsp (2 mL) dried	25 mL

Roll up individual fillets and place seam side down in skillet. Combine fish stock, wine, bay leaf and thyme to make poaching broth. Cover and simmer gently over medium-low heat until cooked (flesh flakes easily when touched with a fork).

Vinaigrette: In a bowl, whisk together olive oil, vinegar, tomato purée, salt, pepper and sugar until well blended and slightly thickened. Add basil and blend.

Place a poached sole fillet on a plate and top with tomato vinaigrette, garnish with fresh herbs and lemon wedges.

Makes 6 servings.

GRILLED SCALLOPS WITH LEMON CHIVE BUTTER

Unlike the rather homely lobster, scallops are found in beautiful shells, often used as "plates" on which the cooked scallop is served. It may take some effort to find scallop shells, but check with a fishmonger. Many people feel that scallops are an expensive treat, but in fact, since there is no waste and the shellfish is so rich, a quarter-pound per person makes a fine meal at a very reasonable price. Bay scallops, found inshore, are smaller and sweeter than the sea scallops that are now finding their way to the fish counter. Digby, Nova Scotia, gives its name to the best of the inshore scallops, which are coveted throughout North America.

Quickly grilling the scallops brings out their sweet flavor.

Lemon Chive Butter:

1½ tsp	butter	7 mL
1	clove garlic, peeled and minced	1
1 tsp	lemon juice, freshly squeezed	5 mL
¼ cup	butter	50 mL
½ tsp	lemon rind	2 mL
½ tsp	white pepper	2 mL
¼ cup	chives, finely minced	50 mL
	Salt to taste	
1 lb	scallops	500 g
1 tbsp	butter	15 mL

Lemon Chive Butter: In a small skillet over low heat, melt 1½ tsp (7 mL) butter, add garlic. Sauté the garlic for 3 minutes or until it is soft but not browned. Add the lemon juice and cook an additional 1 minute; set aside. In a small bowl, cream the butter, lemon rind, pepper, chives and garlic mixture, blending until smooth. Cover with plastic wrap and refrigerate for at least 2 hours or overnight. After the butter mixture has been refrigerated for a couple of hours it may be shaped into a roll or pressed into a mold for serving. Return to the refrigerator until serving time.

In a skillet over medium heat, melt 1 tbsp (15 mL) butter, add scallops and lightly sauté until just fork tender. Place the scallops on warmed serving plate with several pieces of the lemon chive butter on top of them.

Makes 4 servings.

SEAFOOD RISOTTO

During the early part of the twentieth century, Halifax was a major port of entry for waves of immigrants from Europe. Not as well known as Ellis Island in New York harbor, Pier 16 in southend Halifax welcomed more than one million new residents to North America, most of whom went on to inland cities such as Montreal and Toronto. Some stayed in Nova Scotia, including many Italians, from whom this recipe was adapted.

Risotto must be made with Italian rice (arborio is often available). Regular long-grain rice does not develop the creamy consistency needed for the dish.

½ cup	dry white wine	125 mL
2 lb	mussels, scrubbed and bearded	1 kg
24	steamer clams	24
2 tbsp	olive oil	25 mL
24	medium shrimp, peeled and de-veined	24
2	cloves garlic, chopped Freshly ground pepper	2

Risotto:

6 cups	chicken stock and cooking liquid from mussels, combined	1.5 L
½ tsp	saffron threads	2 mL
6 tbsp	vegetable oil	90 mL
1	small onion, peeled and finely chopped	1
2 cups	arborio rice (available in Italian markets and many supermarkets)	500 mL
½ cup	dry white wine	125 mL
2 tbsp	fresh parsley, chopped Salt and pepper	25 mL

Place the white wine and mussels in a large pot with a tight-fitting lid, and steam, covered, over high heat for 5 minutes or until mussels are opened. Discard any mussels that do not open. Remove the mussels from the cooking liquid and set aside in a bowl to cool. When cool, remove the meat from the shells. Discard shells.

Strain the cooking liquid through a double thickness of cheesecloth, and set aside. Remove the mussels from their shells and discard the shells. Heat the olive oil and garlic in a medium skillet over medium heat and sauté the shrimp until they become opaque and pink in colour. Do not overcook. Set aside.

Risotto: Measure out the reserved mussel liquid and add enough chicken stock so that the total is 6 cups (1.5 L). Place in a saucepan, add the saffron and bring to a simmer. In another saucepan, heat the oil. When hot, add the onion and cook until soft. Stir in the rice with a wooden spoon, until it is well coated with the oil. Add wine and stir. Mix in the simmering stock, ½ cup (125 mL) at a time, stirring frequently. Keeping the mixture at a lively simmer, continue adding liquid as the rice absorbs it. Simmer for 20 minutes, or until rice is tender but not mushy. Add some more liquid if necessary. Season with salt and pepper.

Take ½ cup (125 mL) of the remaining stock (or add enough water to make ½ cup liquid) and place in a covered pot with the clams and steam for 5 minutes until clams open, discarding any that do not.

Remove rice to a heated serving bowl, stir in the mussels, the shrimp and the parsley. Set the clams on the rice and serve.

Makes 6 servings.

SHARK MARGARITA

Shark is an inexpensive, abundant and flavorful fish, which is lately finding its way into markets and restaurants. The preparation here is Caribbean in influence – again paying homage to the trade routes that have existed between Nova Scotia and the Islands.

Cooking with medium, not high, heat is important in order to keep the fish from toughening and drying out.

8	shark steaks (1-inch/2.5-cm thick)	8
⅓ cup	lime juice	75 mL
1 tsp	grated lime rind	5 mL
2	cloves garlic, minced	2
¼ tsp	ground ginger	1 mL
½ cup	vegetable oil	125 mL
1 tsp	freshly ground pepper	5 mL
1 tbsp	liquid honey or maple syrup	15 mL

Rinse shark in cold water and pat dry.

In a large bowl, combine lime juice and rind, garlic, ginger, vegetable oil, pepper and honey. Add shark, stirring to coat well. Cover with plastic wrap and marinate at room temperature for 30 minutes or refrigerate for up to 1 hour, turning shark occasionally. Drain shark, reserving marinade. Grill shark steaks 4 inches (10 cm) from medium-hot coals on a barbecue, or broil in oven on a medium-high setting, brushing with reserved marinade, for 5 to 6 minutes per side.

Makes 8 servings.

NEILS HARBOUR SWORDFISH WITH THREE PEPPER SAUCE

Properly prepared swordfish, fresh from the market, is succulent and juicy. Many people who are put off by swordfish haven't had it well cooked. Overdone, it will be dry and unpleasant. Swordfish is widely available beyond Cape Breton's Neils Harbour (population 233), but the recipe was inspired by the fishermen who land their catch there.

1	yellow pepper	1
1	red pepper	1
2	green peppers	2
1 oz	spinach	30 g
1 tbsp	shallots, chopped	15 mL
1 tbsp	lemon juice	15 mL
1½ cups	white wine	375 mL
1½ cups	cream	375 mL
1 lb	butter (unsalted)	500 g
8	swordfish steaks (6 oz/180 g each) boneless and skinless	8

Boil whole yellow, red and green peppers in salted water for 20 minutes. Cool off and peel and discard skins. Cut each pepper into chunks and remove seeds. Purée each different pepper individually in blender and set aside. Blanch spinach and blend with green pepper to obtain a nice green color.

In a skillet over medium heat, combine the shallots, lemon juice and white wine, and reduce mixture by a quarter. Add cream and reduce for an additional 5 to 7 minutes. Cut butter into cubes and add slowly to the mixture, whisking until a smooth sauce is obtained. Divide the butter sauce into 3 equal portions and stir in one of each of the pepper purées into each portion of the butter sauce; purée and keep warm.

Season swordfish with salt and pepper to taste and charbroil or barbecue over medium heat until cooked, about 7 to 10 minutes on each side.

Spoon enough of each pepper sauce to cover the plate and set the fish on top. Pass the rest of the sauces.

Makes 8 servings.

Vegetables

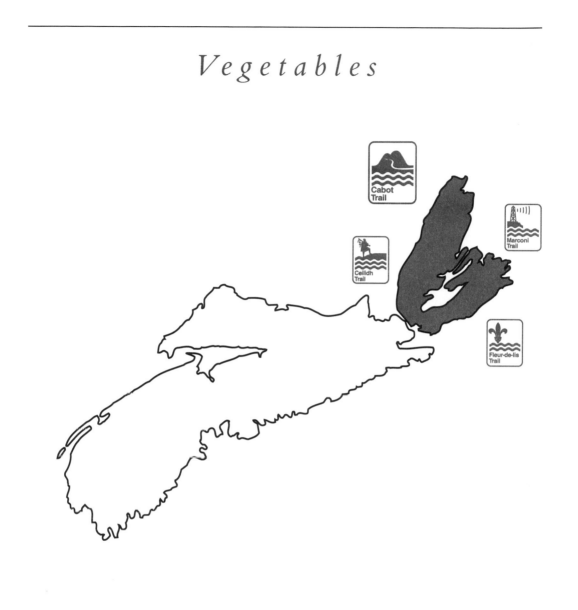

CAPE BRETON ISLAND
AND THE CABOT TRAIL

WESLEY BURTON'S FAMILY SETTLED THE 270-ACRE FARM IN CAPE BRETON'S Margaree Valley four generations ago. Located on a country lane with the unlikely name of the Egypt Road, the Burtons are known throughout the province for the dark, sweet maple syrup that carries the family name. After a long winter marked by storms, snowfall and freezing temperatures the Burtons gear up for an intense few weeks of sugaring.

Many say that there is no real spring on the island, but the syrup makers know that that isn't true. When the daytime temperatures rise above freezing and plummet below the line at night, the maples wake up and the sap starts running.

"We began with 20 taps and buckets, grew after a few years to 200, and collected the sap by horse and sleigh," Wesley recalls. Today they have 1800 taps (on the way to 5000) connected by plastic tubes snaking down the mountain to a central holding tank and a commercial evaporator. "In the old days we had a cement firebox that we filled and refilled with wood to keep the pans of sap boiling day and night." The "sugaring off" took place outside under the sun and stars. When the temperature was just right the sap ran very fast and the cooking went on 24 hours a day. The fire's glow from the meadow announced that it was party time at the Burtons'. Neighbors dropped by, the fiddles appeared and everyone drank sap straight from the bucket – a Cape Breton spring tonic. Eventually a few gallons of rich syrup were poured into gallon jugs; 40 gallons from 200 taps.

Last season, Burton's maple syrup production, using the wood-fired commercial evaporator, was 180 gallons. The Burton children always beg for some of the new syrup to pour on the cold snow and eat as toffee-like candy, as did their great-grandparents before them.

Although the day we visited was hot midsummer, Wesley's reminiscences evoked a Cape Breton April day with crisp air, brilliant sun, deep blue sky and crunchy "corn" snow — the kind that comes from repeated thawing and freezing. It was easy to forget the other Cape Breton April — howling winds, driving snow and icy rains.

The Cape Breton maple syrup is molasses-like in color and very thick. It may not appeal to the refined folks who prefer a lighter variety, but it has a remarkable taste. Wesley's 74-year-old father still works the farm with him. His favorite way to use the syrup is on porridge or as a dip for brown bread. The syrup is distributed in a somewhat haphazard fashion to restaurants, shops and markets around the province. The best way to buy it, however, is to follow the dirt road to the barn and wander around a bit, past the laundry and the cows, calling for Wesley or his father, who sell the syrup and throw in a story or two for free.

Cape Breton Island is home to an amazing mix of people — the Mi'kmaqs, French Acadians and Irish and Scottish immigrants. Each community has maintained its rich culture and unique identity, in part because the Island has been relatively isolated from the mainland of Nova Scotia and the rest of Canada. The causeway connecting Cape Breton to the mainland is less than 40 years old, and before it was built the only way most Islanders could get to the mainland was by ferry.

The Cabot Trail, named for John Cabot, who spotted the Island in 1497 and promptly claimed it for the British crown, is one of the most spectacular drives in North America, with its rollercoaster-like ride over the thousand-foot headlands down to the sea. The mountains of Cape Breton Island are the northernmost tip of the Appalachian chain. From a single vantage point you can spot whales in the Gulf of St. Lawrence, moose in the woods, and eagles and terns soaring high above.

Gaelic, Mi'kmaq, French and English are the living languages of the Island. All are taught in one or another of Cape Breton's schools. Communication between people has been an important part of Cape Breton's heritage. Alexander Graham Bell lived in Baddeck, on Bras d'Or Lake. Marconi's first trans–Atlantic broadcast took place here. The sages of the Island are the storytellers who draw large audiences when they reminisce, keeping history and traditions alive.

All over Cape Breton the arts are a vibrant expression of the island heritage. Music predominates. Teenagers have great respect for the old musicians and are now performing and recording on the fiddle, piano and accordion. Attend one of the frequent barn dances or kitchen parties and you will often see three generations of musicians and dancers joyously performing together. It seems that everyone who plays has a tape for sale between sets or near the punch bowl. Such grassroots marketing keeps the music alive.

The food traditions are down to earth, plain and honest. Great use is made of locally grown, fished and hunted foods – largely because of the expense and difficulty in getting supplies from off the Island. The fact that this is the way tourists like it is not lost on the locals. Chowders, stews, earthy breads and comforting desserts are simple and deliciously cooked in an offhand way that chefs around the world train years to achieve.

APPLE BAKED SQUASH

Squash and apples are two of the treats of the late fall harvest. Baked together, they produce a side dish that is excellent with poultry or pork.

4 cups	acorn, buttercup or other winter squash peeled, seeded and thinly sliced	1 L
3	apples, peeled, cored and thinly sliced	3
¼ cup	butter or margarine	50 mL
¼ cup	apple jelly or marmalade	50 mL
¼ cup	brown sugar	50 mL
1 tsp	salt	5 mL
1 tsp	lemon juice, freshly squeezed	5 mL
¼ tsp	ground cinnamon	1 mL
1	stalk celery, chopped	1

In a greased, 10-inch (25-cm) deep-dish pie plate, arrange the thin slices of squash. Cover with apple slices; set aside. In a small saucepan, melt butter and apple jelly; stir in brown sugar, salt, lemon juice and cinnamon. Pour over squash and apple mixture. Cover and bake in a preheated 350°F (180°C) oven for 45 minutes. Remove from oven and top with chopped celery; return to oven and bake for an additional 5 minutes.

Makes 6 to 8 servings.

DIJON BEETS

Despite their gorgeous color, beets are not usually a popular vegetable unless pickled or made into borscht. This creamy Dijon sauce will make beet lovers out of all. The new golden beets or the candy-striped red and white ones also look great on the plate. All varieties combined make a wildly colored sidedish.

8	red beets	8
1 tbsp	olive oil	15 mL
2 tbsp	onion, finely chopped	25 mL
2 tsp	Dijon mustard	10 mL
¾ cup	sour cream	175 mL
1	sprig fresh dill, chopped fine	1
	Salt and pepper	

Place beets in large saucepan with sufficient water to cover, and bring to boil; reduce to medium heat and cook beets until tender (20 to 30 minutes). Remove from heat, plunge into cold water and remove skin (will fall off easily). Cool beets and then dice into ½-inch (1-cm) pieces.

In a heavy saucepan, heat olive oil over medium heat and add onions, cooking until transparent. Add mustard and sour cream; stir until well blended. Stir in the beets; add salt and pepper to taste. Simmer until beets are heated through (5 to 7 minutes). Remove from heat, place in a serving dish and sprinkle with dill.

Makes 4 to 6 servings.

MASHED POTATOES WITH BAKED GARLIC

Another adaptation of a popular bistro dish, showing a French influence. Slowly baked garlic produces a buttery smooth and sweet pulp which can be served on its own as an unusual side vegetable or can be used in combination with potatoes as shown here. You'll never go back to plain mashed potatoes.

2	bulbs of garlic (not elephant garlic)	2
1 tsp	olive oil	5 mL
8	medium potatoes, peeled and cut into 2-inch (5-cm) pieces	8
1 tsp	salt	5 mL
¾ cup	milk	175 mL
4 tbsp	butter	50 mL
	Salt and freshly ground pepper	
2 tsp	fresh chives, diced (optional)	10 mL

Remove the loose papery skin from the garlic bulbs, leaving the bulb in one piece. Gently rub the garlic with olive oil and set in a small baking dish covered with foil. Bake in a preheated 350°F (180°C) oven for 1 to 1½ hours or until the garlic feels very soft. Remove from the oven and, when cool, squeeze the pulp from the skin and put aside.

In a saucepan, combine salt and sufficient water to cover potatoes and bring to a boil. Add potatoes and return to a boil; reduce heat and simmer until tender (20 to 30 minutes). Just before the potatoes are done, heat the milk (do not boil).

Drain the potatoes and mash with a masher, adding the milk and butter. Mix in the garlic pulp; season with salt and pepper to taste. Stir in chives.

For a variation, substitute 4 tbsp (50 mL) extra virgin olive oil for the butter.

Makes 4 to 6 servings.

POTATOES WITH HORSERADISH BUTTER

What to do with that jar of horseradish that sits in the fridge waiting for a roast beef dinner? Potatoes drizzled with this tangy butter go well with <u>pot roast</u> or other <u>slow-cooked</u> meats, such as <u>lamb shanks</u>.

New potatoes are a real treat, thin-skinned and sweet. It is not necessary to peel them. If they are not available, you may substitute mature potatoes, which should be peeled.

1½ lbs	small potatoes (10)	750 g
⅓ cup	butter	75 mL
1 tbsp	lemon juice, freshly squeezed	15 mL
1 tsp	horseradish	5 mL
2	green onions, chopped	2
¼ tsp	dried dillweed	1 mL
½ tsp	salt	2 mL
	Freshly ground pepper	

Peel potatoes, or scrub if they are new potatoes, place in saucepan with sufficient boiling water to cover, return to boil and cook until done. In a small saucepan, melt butter and stir in lemon juice, horseradish, green onions, dillweed, salt and pepper. Simmer over low heat for 2 minutes. Drain cooked potatoes and place in a serving dish, then pour butter mixture over them. Serve hot.

Makes 4 servings.

POTATO AND SORREL GRATIN

Sorrel, with its tart, lemony flavor, is an underused herb, now available almost everywhere fresh herbs are sold. Combined with nutty Gruyère and garlic, this potato gratin is a flavorful and filling dish. It could be the centerpiece of a light dinner, accompanied by good bread and a salad.

1	garlic clove, peeled	1
2 lb	baking potatoes	1 kg
½ cup	fresh sorrel leaves, finely chopped	125 mL
1 cup	Gruyère cheese, grated	250 mL
1 cup	whipping cream or crème fraîche	250 mL
	Salt and pepper	

Rub a shallow casserole dish (about 6-cup or 1.5-L size) with the garlic clove, then discard garlic. Peel potatoes and thinly slice (by hand or food processor). Wash, drain and chop sorrel. Layer half of the potatoes in the dish; sprinkle with half of the sorrel, as well as half the cheese and cream and a pinch of salt and pepper. Layer the rest of the potatoes, followed by the remainder of the ingredients.

Bake uncovered in a preheated 350°F (180°C) oven for 50 to 60 minutes until golden crust forms.

Makes 4 to 6 servings.

HODGE PODGE

Here is another heritage recipe that has been developed and adapted by Nova Scotian cooks for many generations. Either use fresh vegetables from the garden, or change the recipe according to what is available in the market, just as long as you keep a variety of colors. Avoid overcooking so the taste and texture stay fresh and crisp.

Hodge Podge is an anglicized version of the French Hochepot, which refers to a way of cooking that involves shaking the pan to keep the ingredients from sticking. Feel free to stir rather than shake.

1 cup	small carrots, scrubbed	250 mL
1-2 cups	small new potatoes	250- 500 mL
1 cup	green or wax beans (trimmed, cut into pieces)	250 mL
1 cup	broccoli or cauliflower, coarsely chopped	250 mL
1 cup	sugar snap or snow peas	250 mL
1 cup	shelled peas	250 mL
1 cup	whipping cream or sour cream (light sour cream may be substituted) Salt and pepper	250 mL

In a large saucepan, cook vegetables in salted water until tender crisp. Do not overcook. Start with vegetables that take longer to cook and add others so that all will be tender at the same time. Drain vegetables. Reserve ¼ cup (50 mL) of cooking liquid. Add salt and pepper, whipping cream or sour cream to the cooking liquid and pour over vegetables. Let stand for 15 minutes before serving.

Makes 6 servings.

TANGY BAKED CARROTS

Cooked carrots are possibly not the most popular vegetable around, probably because they are usually overcooked and thrown on a plate for color. This baked version once again finds use for the bite of horseradish. Please try to use homemade "boiled" mayonnaise. If that is not possible use real prepared mayonnaise, not one that is "salad dressing."

4	medium to large carrots	4

"Boiled" Mayonnaise:

2 tbsp	all-purpose flour	25 mL
1 tsp	dry mustard	5 mL
1 tsp	salt	5 mL
⅔ cup	granulated sugar	150 mL
1	egg	1
¾ cup	white vinegar	175 mL
¾ cup	milk	175 mL

Sauce:

½	small onion, finely diced	½
½ cup	mayonnaise	125 mL
½-1 tsp	horseradish (to taste)	2-5 mL
2 tbsp	chopped fresh parsley	25 mL
1 tbsp	water	15 mL

Wash and peel carrots, then slice either on the diagonal or in sticks. Blanch until tender crisp. Place in a greased 4-cup (1-L) casserole dish or pan.

Mayonnaise: In the top portion of a double boiler, whisk together all above ingredients until smooth. Cook in double boiler over medium heat until thick, whisking occasionally.

Sauce: Mix finely diced onion with mayonnaise, horseradish, parsley and water. Pour sauce evenly over carrots. Cover and bake in a preheated oven at 350°F (180°C) for 20 to 25 minutes until carrots are tender crisp.

Makes 4 servings.

Sautéed Fiddleheads and Cranberries

Fiddleheads are the curled-up fronds of the ostrich fern, found in marshy areas in early spring. They are now quick-frozen and available all year round. Many people say that they taste like asparagus, but we think they are "wilder" in taste and texture, making a great combination with the tart cranberry. Be sure to remove the papery outer layer and wash the fiddleheads very well before cooking.

¼ cup	butter	50 mL
8 oz	fiddleheads (washed if fresh)	250 g
¼ cup	fresh or frozen cranberries	50 mL
2 tbsp	maple syrup	25 mL
	Salt	
	Freshly ground pepper	

In a large skillet, melt the butter over medium-high heat. Add the fiddleheads and sauté for 3 minutes or until they begin to soften. Add cranberries and maple syrup and cover, reducing heat to medium, and steam for 3 minutes longer or until tender crisp. Season with salt and freshly ground pepper to taste.

Makes 4 servings.

WARM RED CABBAGE COMPOTE

Hungarian cooks will be familiar with the combination of red cabbage, caraway seeds and sour cream. Our version adds tart apples and is served more undercooked than its Eastern European counterpart.

2 tbsp	olive oil	25 mL
2 tbsp	red wine vinegar	25 mL
1	clove garlic, chopped	1
1	medium onion, thinly sliced	1
1	small red cabbage, quartered, cored and thinly sliced	1
½ tsp	sugar	2 mL
½ tsp	salt	2 mL
¼ tsp	freshly ground pepper	1 mL
1 tsp	caraway seeds	5 mL
1	tart apple, peeled, cored and thinly sliced	1
¼ cup	sour cream	50 mL

In a large skillet, heat oil and red wine vinegar over medium heat; add garlic and onion, sauté until onion becomes soft. Stir in the cabbage, sugar, salt, pepper and caraway seeds and cook over medium heat until cabbage becomes tender crisp. Add sliced apple and sour cream and stir until the sour cream coats the cabbage and apples.

Variation: Include pieces of crisp bacon when adding apple and sour cream.

Makes 6 servings.

MAPLE-GLAZED ONIONS

Maple-glazed onions are like a warm chutney or compote that goes particularly well with red meat.

1 tbsp	butter	15 mL
1 tbsp	red wine	15 mL
2	medium-sized onions, peeled and diced	2
1½ tsp	sugar	7 mL
2 tbsp	maple syrup	25 mL
2 tbsp	celery leaves, chopped	25 mL
2 tbsp	pimento or blanched red pepper, chopped	25 mL

Melt butter in sauté pan; add wine, onions and sugar. Cook over medium-high heat until onions are turning light brown and sugar is caramelized. Stir in maple syrup and cook on high heat for approximately 3 minutes. Remove from heat and add celery leaves and chopped pimento or red peppers.

Makes 4 side servings.

Desserts

Sunrise
Trail

THE SUNRISE TRAIL

Along the shore of the Northumberland Strait is the birthplace of Scottish culture in Nova Scotia. Oddly enough, although the early English explorers had called the land Nova Scotia (New Scotland) from 1621 on, it was not until 1733 that the immigrant ship *Hector* set sail from Scotland and brought the first permanent Scottish settlers to this part of the new world.

They wasted no time. Scottish culture quickly took a leading role in the life of the province. If we were to have an official musical instrument, it would be the bagpipes. Even today, tourists arriving via the only land link to the rest of Canada, located at the head of the Sunrise Trail, are welcomed by a piper parading at the border. We also have an official tartan inspired by our Highland ancestors, and Gaelic, the first language of Scotland, is still spoken in pockets across the province.

The Sunrise Trail was named by the settlers who, after trying more western reaches of Canada, decided to return to the fertile meadows, sandy beaches and warm waters of the Northumberland Shore. They turned east, into the sunrise, and established villages and farms along this north coast. The salt water, warmer here than any place north of the Carolinas, supports rich shellfish grounds.

The Scots were an organized people. In 1817, the West River Farming Society was established and the no-nonsense bylaws included this rule, "If any member shall curse or swear or use any indecent language, or introduce any subject inconsistent with the business of the Society, he shall be fined by the president and a majority of the members present in a sum not exceeding 5s. (shillings)." Those folks meet today as the Pictou Agricultural Society. As one can imagine, they got things done.

Farms were established in the style of the old country, raising dairy cows, planting oats, barley and wheat. Gristmills were built along the streams and rivers, and some still operate today, producing the rough stone-ground flour that makes such wonderfully chewy, flavorful breads. Lobster pounds and shipyards sprang up along the shore.

Great rivalries, some friendly and some not so, existed between the clans in the Highlands and Lowlands of Scotland. The spirit of competition accompanied the immigrants and found a home on the athletic fields. The Annual Highland Games in Antigonish have taken place each summer since 1861 and include traditional contests of heavyweight tossing and lifting by beefy, kilt-clad athletes. Music and dance are a large part of the games and bring the competitors and the observers together on the dance floor.

Hans Jost is not a Scotsman. The Jost family began making wine in Germany, sometime before 1643. His father, Hans Wilhelm Jost, with a "go-west-young-man" spirit, decided to move to North America, settling on a farm in Malagash, Nova Scotia. For sheer beauty, it's no wonder Hans Wilhelm chose Malagash. The drive to the farm takes one over rolling hills mottled with shades of green from the mix of evergreens and hardwood trees, past fields of grain and hay that run right into the sandy beaches at the water's edge and through acres of vines, which in autumn bend under the weight of ripe, sweet grapes. The waters of the Northumberland Strait reflect the bright blue autumn sky and the steely gray of the winter's cloud and fog. If it is very clear you can see Prince Edward Island, Canada's smallest province, lying some 20 miles offshore.

"We didn't plant any grapes at first, because we were told they wouldn't grow," Hans recounted to us in the winery where we were surrounded by thousands of corked bottles.

It didn't make sense to Hans Wilhelm. After all, the climate was relatively mild and there was a long, cool ripening season, extending well into the fall.

Such conditions should be the ideal way to get the right sugar level in the grapes. Given the time, the sugar content slowly builds, being joined with rich flavors from the green plant, the woody vine and the soil. Logically, it should work. Besides, Hans Wilhelm inherited the collective knowledge of his family's 350 years of winemaking experience and he was sure it could be done.

Being a cautious man, Hans Wilhelm worked for years with the agricultural research station in Kentville and in 1978 planted 5 vines from grapes cultivated at the station. The grapes seemed happy enough and the sample wine they produced was quite pleasant. The next year he planted 400 vines. The French and German hybrid grapes, Seyval Blanc, Geisenheim and Marechal Foch, did the best.

"We had more wine than we could drink," said Hans, "and decided to plant enough new vines so that we could go into commercial production. By 1981 we had 4000 vines and are now producing on 600 of our own acres and contract with other growers for additional grapes."

Hans Wilhelm Jost passed away in 1988, after seeing his farm receive a commercial winery license and his product win critical acclaim. His wines have received many medals in wine expositions in North America and Europe. Nova Scotia chefs can now pair local food and wine when presenting their Taste of Nova Scotia menus.

The winery, still experimenting with new varieties, spawned a new industry in Nova Scotia. There are at present four operating wineries in the province. Hans is now working with fruit other than grapes, and has just released a soft apple wine. Hans and his wife, Karen, along with his mother, Erna, still run the operation. Planting, testing, selling, and meeting the thousands of visitors who come to the winery shop. The newest wine, in the style of the German Ice wines, is named after Hans and Karen's second daughter, Matina. It remains a family affair as the Josts close in on 400 years in the business.

APPLE–BERRY CHARLOTTE

The trick is to take apples and berries, the favorite dessert fruits, and find new ways of combining them. The baked Apple–Berry Charlotte is served enticingly warm and garnished with cream.

3	large apples	3
1 cup	fresh or frozen blueberries, strawberries and/or raspberries	250 mL
2 cups	soft white bread crumbs	500 mL
¼ tsp	ground cinnamon	1 mL
½ cup	brown sugar	125 mL
¼ cup	butter	50 mL

Peel, core and slice apples thinly; wash the berries if fresh. Mix bread crumbs with cinnamon and sugar. In a skillet over medium heat, melt butter, and add bread crumbs, stirring until moistened and slightly golden.

Sprinkle a thin layer of crumbs in the bottom of a 9-inch (22-cm) pie plate. Cover with a layer of apples, and then a layer of crumbs. Repeat this twice. Then add a layer of berries, a crumb layer, an apple layer, and top off with crumbs.

Bake in a preheated 350°F (180°C) oven for 50 to 60 minutes until top is golden brown. Serve with fresh cream or custard.

Makes 8 servings

ANNAPOLIS VALLEY APPLE TORTE

***This torte cuts into firm slices, each studded with apples,
and is a fresh change from apple pie.***

Base:

½ cup	butter	125 mL
⅓ cup	granulated sugar	75 mL
¼ tsp	vanilla	1 mL
1 cup	all-purpose flour	250 mL
½ cup	raspberry jam	125 mL

Filling:

1 cup	cream cheese, softened	250 mL
½ cup	granulated sugar	125 mL
1	large egg	1
½ tsp	vanilla	2 mL

Topping:

4 cups	apples, peeled, cored and sliced	1 L
⅓ cup	granulated sugar	75 mL
½ tsp	ground cinnamon	2 mL
½ cup	slivered almonds	125 mL

Cream together butter, sugar and vanilla; add flour and stir until mixture resembles coarse crumbs. Press into bottom and 1 inch (2.5 cm) up the sides of a 9-inch (23-cm) springform pan. Spread raspberry jam on the bottom crust. Mix filling ingredients until smooth, and spread evenly over base. Toss peeled and sliced apples with sugar and cinnamon and arrange gently on filling. Sprinkle with slivered almonds.

Bake in a preheated oven at 400°F (200°C) for 10 minutes. Reduce oven temperature to 350°F (180°C) and continue baking for 30 minutes or until apples are tender. Cool and serve with whipped cream.

Makes 10 to 12 servings.

BLUEBERRY GRUNT

Low-bush blueberries, which are indigenous to Nova Scotia, are the small, wild berries that travelers to New England and the Maritimes often come across when hiking along country roads. We also grow the high-bush variety, which, as the name implies, grow on bushes 4 to 6 feet (1.2 to 1.8 m) tall.

Blueberry Grunt is another of our old recipes. There is likely to be a grunt recipe in every local cookbook. Serve it once and it will become a much-requested favorite.

Sauce:

4 cups	fresh or frozen blueberries	1 L
½ tsp	ground nutmeg	2 mL
½ tsp	ground cinnamon	2 mL
¾ cup	granulated sugar	175 mL
1 tbsp	lemon juice	15 mL
½ cup	water	125 mL

Dumplings:

2 cups	all-purpose flour	500 mL
4 tsp	baking powder	20 mL
½ tsp	salt	2 mL
1 tbsp	granulated sugar	15 mL
2 tbsp	butter or shortening	25 mL
	Milk	

In a large saucepan with cover, heat berries, nutmeg, cinnamon, sugar, lemon juice and water; boil gently until well blended and slightly cooked down.

In a mixing bowl, sift flour, baking powder, salt and sugar. Cut in butter and add enough milk to make a soft biscuit dough. Drop by spoonfuls into hot berry sauce. Cover tightly with a lid and simmer for 15 minutes (no peeking!). The dumplings should be puffed and well cooked. Transfer cooked dumplings to serving dish. Ladle sauce over top; serve with whipped cream. Scrumptious!

Makes 6 to 8 servings.

BREAD PUDDING

New Orleans restaurants are justifiably proud of their homey bread puddings. We know that the tradition was brought to Lousiana by Acadians from Nova Scotia (who became known as "Cajuns"), so we'll take some of the credit. Once you've made this pudding, you'll never have a reason to throw away stale bread again. Just pop a bag into the freezer and, when you have accumulated enough, make a pan of bread pudding. This is one recipe that requires a stale ingredient, so be patient and start your collection.

8 cups	any type of stale bread, cake or cookies, crumbled	2 L
4 cups	milk	1 L
2 cups	granulated sugar	500 mL
3	eggs	3
2 tbsp	vanilla	25 mL
1 cup	raisins or currants	250 mL
1 cup	walnuts, chopped and toasted	250 mL
1 tsp	ground cinnamon	5 mL
1 tsp	ground nutmeg	5 mL
1 tsp	ground mace	5 mL
½ cup	melted butter	125 mL

Combine all ingredients in a large mixing bowl. Mixture should be very moist but not soupy. Pour into a buttered 12- x 10-inch (32- x 26-cm) baking dish. Place in a cold oven. Turn oven on to 350°F (180°C) and bake until golden brown, about 1¼ hours. Serve warm with your favourite sauce.

Hint: This bread pudding freezes very well. If you plan to freeze it, make your batter a little moister.

Makes 8 to 10 servings.

Strawberry Sauce:

4 cups	fresh or frozen strawberries	1 L
2 tbsp	Cointreau or Tia Maria liqueur	25 mL
½ cup	granulated sugar	125 mL
1 tbsp	cornstarch	15 mL
2 tbsp	cold water	25 mL

In saucepan, combine strawberries, liqueur and sugar. Cover and cook for 8 to 10 minutes over medium heat. Mix cornstarch with cold water; stir into strawberry mixture. Cook 2 minutes. Remove from heat and cool.

Whiskey Sauce:

½ cup	butter	125 mL
1½ cup	icing sugar	375 mL
2	egg yolks	2
½ cup	whiskey or brandy	125 mL

In a saucepan over medium heat, melt butter, whisk in sugar until dissolved. Remove from heat and whisk in egg yolks. Gradually pour whiskey and stir constantly until well blended. Sauce will thicken as it cools. Serve sauce warm over bread pudding.

CAPE BRETON PORK PIES

Pork pie for dessert? When the "pork" is really chopped dates it works well. There are a million stories about the origin of the name, none of which we believe, so we'll have to keep guessing. This is a rich dessert, but the small tart shell only offers a few bites.

Shortbread Shells:

1 cup	butter	250 mL
½ cup	icing sugar, sifted	125 mL
1	egg yolk	1
1 tsp	vanilla	5 mL
2 cups	all-purpose flour	500 mL
2 tbsp	cornstarch	25 mL
¼ tsp	salt	1 mL

Filling:

2¼ cups	chopped dates	550 mL
¾ cup	packed brown sugar	175 mL
¾ cup	boiling water	175 mL
¼ tsp	salt	1 mL
1 tsp	vanilla	5 mL

Icing:

⅔ cup	icing sugar, sifted	150 mL
2 tbsp	maple syrup	25 mL
1 tbsp	butter, softened	15 mL

Shortbread shells: In large bowl, cream butter with sugar until fluffy; beat in egg yolk and vanilla. Sift together flour, cornstarch and salt; gradually stir into creamed mixture, gently kneading until smooth.

Working in batches, gently form dough into ¾-inch (2-cm) balls, place in 1½-inch (4-cm) tart cups and press evenly over bottom and sides of cup to form shell. Bake in 325°F (160°C) oven for about 18 minutes or until crisp and pale golden. Let cool in pan on rack; loosen shells with tip of knife.

Filling: In a small saucepan, bring dates, sugar, water and salt to boil over medium heat; reduce heat and simmer, stirring often, for 4 minutes or until thickened and smooth. Let cool; stir in vanilla. Spoon into shells.

Icing: Blend together icing sugar, maple syrup and butter until smooth; place a dollop onto each tart. (Tarts can be stored at room temperature for up to 4 days or frozen for up to 2 weeks.)

Makes 4 dozen.

CRANACHAN

Cranachan traveled from the Highlands of Scotland to the Highlands of Cape Breton Island. It was served traditionally as a dessert on Christmas Day. The toasted oats bring a nutty crunch to the whipped cream and fresh fruit.

1 cup	whipping cream	250 mL
¼ cup	icing sugar	50 mL
½ tsp	vanilla	2 mL
½ cup	oatmeal, toasted	125 mL
1 cup	fresh fruit	250 mL
	Dark rum (optional)	

Preheat oven to 350°F (180°C). Place oatmeal on a baking pan in a thin layer and bake for 10 minutes until nut-brown.

In a mixing bowl, whip cream until firm, but not dry. To whipping cream, gently add icing sugar, vanilla and oatmeal. Spoon mixture into 4 individual serving dishes; top with fresh fruit of your choice (blueberries, strawberries or raspberries). For an extra touch, drizzle with dark rum. Garnish with fresh mint or a piece of the fresh fruit.

Makes 4 servings.

CARROT TORTE

Carrot Torte is a flourless cake, bound together by ground almonds and richly flavored with cinnamon, cloves and cherry-scented kirsch. The cake stays moist for a couple of days if well covered.

5	egg yolks (reserve the whites)	5
1½ cups	sugar	375 mL
1	lemon, juice and grated rind	1
2⅔ cups	ground almonds	650 mL
3 cups	carrots, finely grated	750 mL
⅔ cups	cornstarch	150 mL
pinch	ground cinnamon	pinch
pinch	ground cloves	pinch
pinch	salt	pinch
2½ tsp	baking powder	12 mL
5	egg whites, stiffly beaten	5
¼ cup	kirsch	50 mL
½ cup	apricot jam	125 mL

Beat egg yolks, sugar, lemon juice and grated rind until mixture is spongy in texture. Fold in almonds and grated carrots. Add the cornstarch, cinnamon, cloves, salt and baking powder. Mix together lightly but well. In another bowl beat egg whites until stiff peak forms. Gently fold in egg whites and kirsch.

Line a 10-inch (25-cm) spring-form pan with greased wax paper. Pour dough into pan and bake in a preheated 350°F (180°C) oven for 50 to 60 minutes or until top is light golden brown. Remove from oven and, while still hot, brush with heated apricot jam.

Makes 8 to 12 servings.

MAPLE MOUSSE

Many mousse purists wouldn't consider marrying the eggs and cream to anything but fine chocolate. Trust us, pure maple syrup is a wonderful alternative.

For an extra-special dessert, poach some whole, peeled pears in enough water, red or white wine to cover them, along with two tablespoons of sugar. When the pears are tender, remove them from the liquid and serve with the maple mousse.

6	egg yolks	6
¾ cup	pure maple syrup	175 mL
	Dash of salt	
2 cups	whipping cream	500 mL

Combine egg yolks, maple syrup and salt in top of double boiler and cook until thickened, stirring constantly (approximately 10 to 15 minutes). When custard coats the back of a spoon, remove from heat. Pour into a large bowl and beat with wire whisk until cooled – custard will appear light and frothy. Set aside. Meanwhile, place the whipping cream in a large bowl, and whip until thickened, but not stiff. Fold gently into custard until blended. Pour into 8 individual serving dishes or molds and place in freezer for at least 6 hours. Remove when ready to serve and garnish with whipped cream and fresh mint leaf.

Makes 8 servings.

PUMPKIN CHEESECAKE

Howard Dill's award-winning pumpkins have come from the soils of Windsor in the Annapolis Valley. Mr. Dill has grown pumpkins that tip the scales at 700 lb – that's a lot of pumpkin pie or cheesecake. (In fact a pumpkin weighing just under 500 lb once made 442 pumpkin pies.) Howard Dill now markets the "Dill Atlantic Giant" pumpkin seeds so that you can grow your own giant pumpkins. Fortunately, you do not need a giant pumpkin to make this luscious cheesecake.

Crust:

2 cups	graham wafer crumbs	500 mL
¼ cup	butter, softened	50 mL

Filling:

1½ lb	cream cheese	750 g
1 cup	granulated sugar	250 mL
1½ tsp	ground cinnamon	7 mL
1 tsp	ground nutmeg	5 mL
½ tsp	ground clove	2 mL
4	eggs	4
1½ cups	pumpkin, puréed	375 mL

Crust: In a small mixing bowl, blend together graham cracker crumbs and butter. Press crust mixture on the bottom and up the sides of a 9-inch (23-cm) springform pan. Chill until filling is ready.

Filling: Divide filling ingredients into roughly three portions and mix each portion in a food processor until smooth. Pour each portion into a large bowl as done. Mix all portions together with a hand mixer until smooth and well blended. Pour into springform pan. Bake in preheated oven at 275°F (140°C) for 2½ hours. Cool to room temperature before refrigerating. Top with fresh whipped cream and garnish with whole almonds.

Makes 12 servings.

SQUASH PIE

Butternut squash has a different flavor and texture from pumpkin's. It is firmer and not as sweet. Pumpkin may be substituted, but try squash first – you'll be pleasantly surprised. To use fresh squash, prepare it for baking by following the same method as for fresh pumpkin on page 18.

2 cups	butternut squash or pumpkin, cooked and mashed*	500 mL
1½ cups	evaporated milk	375 mL
2	eggs	2
¾ cup	brown sugar	175 mL
1½ tsp	ground cinnamon	7 mL
½ tsp	ground ginger	2 mL
½ tsp	ground nutmeg	2 mL
½ tsp	salt	2 mL
¼ cup	whipping cream (optional)	50 mL

In a large bowl, add squash, milk, eggs, sugar and spices, mixing at medium speed until well blended. Pour mixture into a 10-inch (25-cm) pastry-lined pie pan. (See recipe for pie crust on p. 44.) Bake in a preheated 400°F (200°C) oven for 60 minutes or until a knife inserted 1 inch (2.5 cm) from edge comes out clean. Shield crust with foil for last 20 minutes of baking. Cool on a wire rack.

To garnish, whip cream in a small bowl with a mixer on medium speed until stiff peaks form. Serve each slice of pie with a dab of whipped cream.

* Two 400 g packages of frozen, mashed squash may be substituted. Strain excess liquid off until you have 2 cups (500 mL) of pulp.

Makes 8 servings.

STRAWBERRY SHERBET

When local strawberries are in season we come back from a day in the country or a trip to the farmer's market with flats of this irresistibly sweet, juicy fruit. This sherbet is a way to use the berries that aren't perfectly shaped enough to be used in a shortcake or pie.

Blueberries and raspberries also make good sherbet and can be substituted in part or altogether for the strawberries.

2 cups	water	500 mL
1 cup	granulated sugar	250 mL
4 tsp	corn syrup	20 mL
4 cups	strawberries	1 L
2 tbsp	lemon juice	25 mL

In a saucepan, bring water, sugar and corn syrup to boil over high heat, stirring to dissolve sugar; boil for 1 minute. Let cool.

Purée berries in food mill, blender or food processor; combine with sugar mixture and lemon juice. Pour into shallow cake pan; freeze until firm, about 4 hours. Purée in food processor until smooth and creamy; pack into airtight container and refreeze for 4 hours or until firm.

Makes 6 cups (1.5 L).

RHUBARB AND RASPBERRY TART

Raspberries and rhubarb in one tart means that one of the fruits must be frozen if locally produced fruits are to be used. Happily this dish works well with either fresh or frozen berries or rhubarb. The reds and pinks are beautiful together and the flavors blend wonderfully.

2 cups	rhubarb	500 mL
1 cup	raspberries	250 mL
¾ cup	granulated sugar	175 mL
3	eggs	3
1	egg yolk	1
½ cup	whipping cream	125 mL
¼ tsp	vanilla	1 mL
	Pie dough for 10-inch (25-cm) shell	

Roll out pie dough into 10-inch (25-cm) tart or pie pan.

Cut rhubarb into ¼-inch (0.6-cm) pieces, distribute evenly in tart shell, then sprinkle with raspberries.

Combine sugar, eggs and egg yolk in a mixing bowl; whisk ingredients together. Add cream and vanilla and mix. Pour egg mixture over fruit and bake in preheated 400°F (200°C) oven for 20 to 25 minutes, or until tart batter is quite firm.

Makes 8 servings.

Photo: Summerberry Shortcake,
Annapolis Valley Apple Torte
PC 105

SUMMERBERRY SHORTCAKE

It's almost overwhelming to use three different berries for the shortcake topping, but the result is a grand dish with much color and flavor. Most people have it for dessert, but someone we know has convinced us that eating Summerberry Shortcake for an occasional lunch or dinner is therapeutic.

1 cup	raspberries, fresh or frozen	250 mL
1¼ cups	strawberries, sliced	300 mL
1 cup	blueberries	250 mL
1½ cup	apple juice	375 mL
pinch	ground cinnamon	pinch
pinch	ground cloves	pinch
¼ cup	granulated sugar	50 mL
3 tbsp	cornstarch	45 mL

In a saucepan, combine raspberries, strawberries and blueberries (if using frozen fruit thaw and drain) with apple juice, reserving 3 tbsp (45 mL) of apple juice for later use. Add spices and sugar, and cook over low heat for 20 minutes. Combine cornstarch with reserved apple juice to make a paste, gradually add to fruit mixture, stirring constantly until dissolved and mixture thickens. Cool and serve over shortcake.

Shortcake:

2 cups	all-purpose flour	500 mL
4 tsp	baking powder	20 mL
1 tbsp	granulated sugar	15 mL
½ tsp	salt	2 mL
½ cup	shortening or margarine	125 mL
1	egg	1
⅓ cup	milk	75 mL
⅓ cup	sour cream	75 mL

In a mixing bowl, combine flour, baking powder, sugar and salt. Cut in shortening or margarine until well mixed. In a small bowl, combine egg, milk and sour cream; add to flour mixture until well blended. Turn out onto a floured surface and roll out to 1-inch (2.5-cm) thickness and cut into 2-inch (5-cm) rounds. Bake in a preheated 375°F (190°C) oven for 10 to 15 minutes or until golden brown.

To serve, top warm or cooled biscuits with summerberry sauce and, if desired, whipped cream.

Makes 8 to 10 servings.

Photo: The warm, sunny days and cool nights of September ripen the apples to crisp perfection.

IRISH APPLE CAKE

A very comforting dessert. Irish Apple Cake is a fragrant, apple-filled pastry that is also great as an afternoon snack with tea or coffee.

2 cups	all-purpose flour	500 mL
½ tsp	baking powder	2 mL
¼ cup	granulated sugar	50 mL
½ cup	butter	125 mL
1	egg	1
½ cup	milk (more if necessary)	125 mL
3-4	large cooking apples, peeled, cored and sliced	3-4
¼ tsp	ground cloves	1 mL
¼ tsp	ground nutmeg	1 mL
2 tbsp	granulated sugar	25 mL
1	egg beaten (egg wash)	1

In a mixing bowl, sift together flour, baking powder and sugar. Cut in butter with pastry blender. In a small bowl, beat together egg and milk. Add egg mixture to flour mixture and stir to make a soft dough. Divide dough into 2 equal portions. Place one portion in a greased 9-inch (23-cm) pie plate. Pat out with your fingers to cover bottoms and sides. Slightly beat an egg to form an egg wash. Brush egg wash on bottom crust. Arrange apple slices on dough base, and sprinkle with cloves, nutmeg and sugar. Roll out the remaining dough on a floured piece of wax paper until large enough to cover apples and base. Invert the rolled-out dough over the pie plate and peel the wax paper off. Press the edges together. Brush the top crust with remaining egg wash and sprinkle with granulated sugar.

Bake in a preheated 375°F (190°C) oven for 10 minutes, then lower heat to 350°F (180°C) and bake an additional 30 minutes or until golden brown. Top with whipped cream and serve while still warm.

Makes 8 servings.

Breads

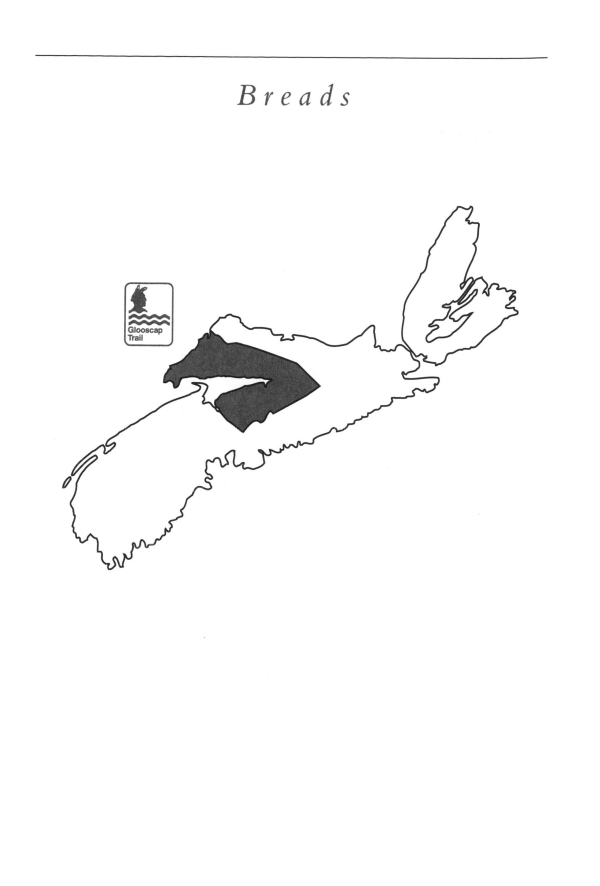

Glooscap
Trail

THE GLOOSCAP TRAIL

THE BAY OF FUNDY GIVES WESTERN NOVA SCOTIA THE HIGHEST, MOST POWERFUL tides in the world. The Mi'kmaqs tell us that Glooscap, the god-chief, created the tides from his vantage point on the summit of Blomidon Mountain overlooking the bay. As the bay narrows, the tide rises higher and increases in speed, creating tidal bores much like small tidal waves, often viewed by many along the shore. For the more adventurous, tour operators offer rubber-raft trips, which give you the chance to ride the crest of the tidal bore.

The tides are not the only legacy of Glooscap. Explorers hiking along the shoreline carved out by the surging water find an abundance of sparkling jasper, agate, amethyst and onyx, all strewn by the chief as a gift to his grandmother.

The Mi'kmaq residing in this part of Nova Scotia did not farm the land intensively, but focussed more on hunting and fishing. Many of our cooking styles were adapted from Mi'kmaq discoveries. They perfected the use of smoking as a means of preserving meat and seafood. They also learned to use the sap of the maple and yellow birch as a natural sweetener. Wild blueberries, huckleberries and cranberries were collected, formed into little cakes and left in the hot sun to dry.

The Glooscap trail, twisting toward the salt water of the Bay of Fundy and suddenly turning back to the rising hills, leads the traveler to the heart of Nova Scotia blueberry production. Blueberries are the most valuable export crop of the province. Generations of farmers worked and harvested the blueberry fields after they discovered the ease with which the berry bush grew in the acidic soil, left behind during the ice age after the huge glaciers from the Arctic finished their slide over Nova Scotia. This soil is not so hospitable to other crops but is a blueberry's preferred home.

"My grandfather told me that every living creature loves blueberries; people, dogs, bears, raccoons, deer, birds and probably even snakes." David Dickenson and his wife Karen live in Southampton where they are the fifth generation of Dickensons to farm the land. The farm, proud recipient of a "Century Farm" designation in 1967, is set in the rolling hills of Cumberland County, where blueberry fields cover the landscape.

The Dickensons arrived in Nova Scotia as part of the immigration wave of the 1850s. On the farm, with its postcard-perfect white clapboard farmhouse set under a long row of maples planted as a windbreak by one of his ancestors, David and Karen also grow strawberries, carrots and feed grain, and produce maple syrup. But blueberries are the primary crop, as they have been for almost 150 years for the Dickensons and their neighbors.

"Even in the early days a lot of our blueberries were sent by train to Boston and New York. To keep them fresh, blocks of ice were stacked outside the rail cars, creating refrigerator cars." The British also developed a taste for the blue colonial berry, but stubbornly refused to call it by its North American name. Invoices for the fruit read "blueberries," but payment notations were for "billberries."

It is not unusual for three generations of pickers to be together in the fields during harvest time. "This year for the first time our 67-year-old neighbor didn't join her daughter and granddaughter in the fields for the harvest, but only because of doctor's orders. We take our crop to the receiving shed near the barn and add it to the production of 20 of our neighbors. What we don't keep for ourselves goes to a processor for shipment to the U.S., Germany or Japan, the new, hot market."

Harvesting blueberries, which grow on low bushes close to the ground, has always been a labor-intensive process. Even in this age of sophisticated mechanical farm equipment, two-thirds of the Dickensons' crop is harvested by hand-raking. A blueberry rake resembles a large comb with a handle that the pickers pull through the blueberry plant from the ground up (literally combing the blueberries off the plants). Varieties of highbush blueberries, growing six feet off the ground and easier to reach, are now being widely cultivated, and are much easier to pick.

Today, city folk have the opportunity to pick berries at one of the many "U-Pick" fields that farmers have opened to their urban cousins. For three weeks or so in August the roadside shoulders are crowded with cars from town, and the fields are filled with an army of weekend farmers. The work of harvesting is fun when you only want a few pints of berries and when the outing is as much the point as the results. Part of the blueberry's popularity stems from the fact that its flavor is remarkably adaptable, ranging from tart to sweet. It is used for every course of the meal, from soup to salad to entrée, as well as bread and desserts.

After the ripe berries are harvested, the green leaves of the bushes turn vibrant red, a harbinger of the brilliant autumn colors that will soon emerge in the woods.

OLD-TIME BANNOCK

*Bannock is a dense and chewy bread that the Scots were very fond of.
We like it hot from the oven with butter and a bowl of soup. Those with a
sweet tooth might like to try it with a little molasses.*

2½ cups	all-purpose flour	625 mL
2 tsp	baking powder	10 mL
3 tbsp	granulated or brown sugar or liquid honey	45 mL
½ tsp	salt	2 mL
2 tbsp	shortening or lard	25 mL
1	egg, slightly beaten	1
	Water	

In a mixing bowl, combine flour, baking powder, sugar and salt. Cut in shortening with fork or pastry blender. Add egg and sufficient water to make a firm dough.

Turn onto a floured board and lightly knead. Place in a lightly buttered 8-inch (20-cm) square baking pan. Bake in preheated 375°F (190°C) oven for 20 minutes.

Makes 9 servings.

BLUEBERRY JOHNNYCAKE

Johnnycake is similar to cornbread and is delicious served with a stew or a chili. The addition of blueberries is an unusual twist.

1 cup	all-purpose flour	250 mL
¾ cup	cornmeal	175 mL
1 tbsp	baking powder	15 mL
½ tsp	salt	2 mL
¼ cup	granulated sugar	50 mL
¼ cup	shortening	50 mL
1	egg, slightly beaten	1
1 cup	milk	250 mL
½ cup	blueberries*	125 mL

In a mixing bowl, blend together flour, cornmeal, baking powder, salt and sugar. Cut in shortening with a pastry blender or fork. Combine beaten egg and milk and add to dry ingredients. Stir until just blended, then gently fold in blueberries. Pour batter into a lightly greased 8-inch (20-cm) square pan and bake in a preheated 375°F (190°C) oven for 25 minutes.

* Blueberries are optional and may be omitted to make a more traditional johnnycake.

Makes 9 servings.

MOLASSES OAT BREAD

This bread is rich with oats and cornmeal and raises into dark-brown and somewhat sweet loaves. It is the kind of bread that is best eaten warm from the oven but also makes excellent toast.

1 cup	rolled oats	250 mL
½ cup	cornmeal	125 mL
1¼ cup	molasses	300 mL
½ tsp	salt	2 mL
2 cups	hot water	500 mL
1½ tbsp	shortening	20 mL
3 tbsp	dry yeast	45 mL
½ tbsp	granulated sugar	7 mL
1 cup	warm water	250 mL
7 cups	all-purpose flour	1.75 L

In a large mixing bowl, combine rolled oats, cornmeal, molasses, salt, hot water and shortening; stir to dissolve shortening. Let cool until lukewarm in temperature. In a small bowl, combine dry yeast, sugar and warm water, cover and let rise until foamy; stir to ensure yeast is dispersed. Blend together yeast and oat mixture. Add half the flour, and mix well; add remaining flour, continuing to mix until the dough begins to come clean from the sides of the bowl but is not dry. Knead for approximately 5 minutes until flour has been uniformly mixed in and the dough is elastic.

Divide dough into 4 equal portions and shape into loaves. Using 2 greased 10- x 16-inch (25- x 40-cm) loaf pans,* place 2 loaves per pan to form double loaves. Cover and set aside to rise in a warm place until dough is approximately double in size (about 1 to 1½ hours). Bake in a preheated 350°F (180°C) oven for 25 to 30 minutes or until loaves sound hollow when tapped.

* *A cooking spray may be used to grease pans and to lightly spray loaves.*

Makes 2 double loaves.

FOCACCIA

Italians are a small but active ethnic group in Nova Scotia. We have them to thank for the focaccia, the soft herb bread available at the Halifax Farmer's Market, in many bakeries and now, frozen in the supermarkets. A great sandwich consists of focaccia sliced horizontally and filled with roasted sweet pepper, fresh mozzarella (also available in many markets) and a few large basil leaves.

2 cups	warm milk	500 mL
1 tsp	granulated sugar	5 mL
2 tsp	dried oregano	10 mL
2 tsp	dried basil	10 mL
2 tsp	dried thyme or rosemary	10 mL
2 tsp	dried parsley	10 mL
1 tsp	black pepper	5 mL
1 tbsp	dry yeast	15 mL
2 tsp	salt	10 mL
3 cups	all-purpose flour	750 mL
¾ cup	olive oil	175 mL
½ cup	yellow onion, peeled and finely chopped	125 mL

In a large mixing bowl, combine warm milk, sugar, herbs, pepper and yeast. Cover with a tea towel and let rise for 5 minutes or until foamy. To yeast mixture, add salt and flour; stir until blended. Add ½ cup (125 mL) olive oil and chopped onion to dough; stir until blended. Cover and set aside to let rise for 1 hour or until double in size.

Punch dough down and stir in remaining ¼ cup (50 mL) olive oil. The dough will be quite sticky. On a greased 17- x 12-inch (42- x 30-cm) cookie sheet, spread dough out. (Oil your fingers lightly so dough will not stick to them.) Cover and let rise for 30 minutes. Bake in a preheated 400°F (200°C) oven for 30 minutes.

HERB BREAD

Here is another version of a herb bread, somewhat like the foccacia but one that bakes into a chewier and more textured loaf.

1½ tbsp	yeast	20 mL
3 tbsp	granulated sugar	45 mL
1 cup	warm water	250 mL
2 tbsp	shortening	25 mL
1 tbsp	salt	15 mL
1 cup	warm milk	250 mL
3 tbsp	herbs (basil, marjoram, poppyseed, garlic powder). If using fresh herbs increase to ⅓ cup (75 mL)	45 mL
9 cups	all-purpose flour	2.25 L
1-2 cups	lukewarm water, just enough to moisten	250-500 mL
2 tbsp	poppyseeds	30 mL

In a small mixing bowl, dissolve yeast and sugar in warm water and let rise until foamy. In a large mixing bowl, blend shortening, salt, warm milk and herbs. Add yeast mixture, blending well. Add 4 cups (1 L) flour and 1 cup (250 mL) water, mix well and then add 3 cups (750 mL) flour and ½ cup (125 mL) water, and stir until well blended. Stir in remaining 2 cups (500 mL) of flour to form soft dough, adding remaining water if needed. Turn dough onto floured work surface and knead until dough is smooth and elastic. Place dough in an oiled bowl, cover and let rise in a warm place for 1½ hours or until double in size.

Punch dough down and divide into 5 equal portions, place in greased 8- x 4-inch (20- x 10-cm) bread pans, sprinkle top with poppy seeds. Cover and let rise for 1½ hours or until double in size. Bake in preheated 325°F (160°C) oven for 35 to 40 minutes or until golden brown.

Makes 5 loaves.

OATCAKES

Oatcakes are good at both teatime and breakfast. They are like oatmeal cookies, but not as sweet and with a much more delicate texture. Many restaurants include oatcakes in their dinner bread baskets and they are often the first bread munched on. Another reason to be grateful to our Scottish ancestors.

3 cups	rolled oats	750 mL
1½ cups	all-purpose flour	375 ml
½ cup	packed brown sugar	125 mL
½ tsp	salt	2 mL
½ tsp	baking soda	2 mL
1 cup	shortening	250 mL
½ cup	cold water	125 mL

In a large bowl, sift together oats, flour, sugar, salt and baking soda. With pastry blender, cut in shortening until crumbly. Gradually sprinkle mixture with water, tossing with fork to make a sticky dough. Gather into ball; divide in half.

On floured pastry cloth and using floured rolling pin, roll out each half to a 12- x 9-inch (30- x 23-cm) rectangle. Cut into 3-inch (8-cm) squares; cut each diagonally in half if desired.

Bake on greased baking sheets in 350°F (180°C) oven for 10 to 15 minutes or until oatcakes are golden brown on bottom. Transfer to racks and let cool.

Makes 24 oatcakes.

PORRIDGE BREAD

A wonderfully fragrant, soft brown bread, porridge bread uses leftover oatmeal for taste and texture. (If oatmeal is not so popular at your home just make it for the bread and skip the "leftover" step.) Don't forget to read the French Toast recipe on page 150 which calls for porridge bread. You may have to hide some away in order to have enough for the French Toast.

Porridge:

3 cups	boiling water	750 mL
¾ tsp	salt	3 mL
1⅓ cups	rolled oats	325 mL

Bread:

1 cup	warm water	250 mL
1½ tsp	granulated sugar	7 mL
4 tsp	dry yeast	20 mL
2 cups	porridge	500 mL
½ cup	brown sugar	125 mL
¾ cup	vegetable oil	175 mL
½ cup	molasses	125 mL
7 cups	all-purpose flour	1750 mL
1½ tsp	salt	7 mL

In a saucepan, bring water and salt to a boil; add rolled oats and bring back to a boil, stirring frequently. Remove from heat and set porridge aside. In a small mixing bowl, dissolve sugar in warm water; add yeast and let rise until foamy. In a large mixing bowl, blend together porridge, brown sugar, oil and molasses. To porridge mixture, add yeast mixture, stirring to combine. Add flour 1 cup at a time, stirring to blend well, and continue to add flour until dough starts to come clean from the sides of the bowl but is not dry. Turn onto a floured surface and knead until dough is smooth and somewhat elastic. Cover and let rise in a warm place until double in size (60 to 90 minutes).

Punch dough down and divide into 6 equal pieces. Shape into loaves and place 2 loaves each into 3 greased 10- x 6-inch (25- x 15-cm) double bread pans. Cover and set aside to rise in a warm draft-free place until double in size, approximately 1 hour. Bake in a preheated 325°F (160°C) oven for 30 to 40 minutes or until loaves are golden brown.

Makes 3 double loaves.

SCONES

Scones are a very popular teatime treat that are often served with clotted cream and homemade strawberry jam. As this variation of the recipe shows, the basic dough can make a nice biscuit to accompany a meal.

3 cups	all-purpose flour	750 mL
3 tbsp	granulated sugar	45 mL
4 tsp	baking powder	20 mL
½ tsp	salt	2 mL
½ cup	shortening	125 mL
1	egg, slightly beaten	1
1 cup	milk	250 mL
1 cup	raisins	250 mL

In a mixing bowl, combine flour, sugar, baking powder and salt; cut in shortening with a pastry blender. Add beaten egg and milk to mixture to form a soft dough. Blend in raisins.* On a floured surface, turn out dough and pat or roll out to ¾-inch (2-cm) thickness. Cut into rounds, place on baking pan and brush top with milk, then sprinkle with granulated sugar. Bake in a preheated 400°F (200°C) oven for 15 minutes.

Variation: You can omit raisins and use as biscuits, or replace raisins with ½ cup (125 mL) grated cheddar cheese.

Makes approximately 2 dozen.

SOURDOUGH MULTIGRAIN SEED BREAD

Sourdough breads need a "starter" to begin from. Those unfamiliar with the sourdough process will be surprised to find the starter so easy to make. The sunflower, sesame and flax seeds make the bread very chewy and give a nutty flavour.

2½ tbsp	dry yeast	35 mL
1 tbsp	granulated sugar	15 mL
1 cup	warm water	250 mL
1¼ cup	sourdough starter (see page 133)	300 mL
2 tbsp	salt	30 mL
¾ cup	liquid honey	175 mL
½ cup	sunflower seeds	125 mL
½ cup	sesame seeds	125 mL
½ cup	flax seeds	125 mL
5¼ cups	water	1.3 L
6 cups	whole wheat flour	1.5 L
5 cups	all purpose flour	1.2 L

In a small mixing bowl, dissolve yeast and sugar in warm water. Cover and let rise for 5 minutes or until yeast is foamy.

In a large mixing bowl, combine sourdough starter, salt, honey, seeds and yeast mixture; stir until well blended. Add ½ cup (125 mL) each of whole wheat flour, white flour and water; stir until smooth. Add remaining flour and water 1 cup (250 mL) at a time to form a soft dough. Turn dough onto floured work surface and knead for 5 minutes. Place dough in an oiled bowl, sprinkle with whole wheat flour (approximately ½ cup, or 125 mL), cover and let rise for 1½ hours.

Punch down and knead lightly. Divide dough into 5 equal portions. Shape into loaves and place in 8- x 4-inch (20- x 10-cm) greased loaf pans. Cover and let rise in a warm, draft-free place for 1½ hours. Bake in a preheated 450°F (230°C) oven for 20 minutes, reduce temperature to 375°F (190°C) and bake an additional 25 to 30 minutes. Remove from pans and let cool on racks.

Yields 5 medium-sized loaves.

Photo: Blueberry Johnnycake, Oatcakes, assorted preserves

Sourdough Starter:

½ tsp	dry yeast	2 mL
¼ cup	warm water	50 mL
1¼ cup	water	325 mL
2 tbsp	water	30 mL
3¾ cup	all-purpose flour	925 mL

Mix yeast with warm water. Let set while you mix 1¼ cup (325 mL) plus 2 tbsp (25 mL) water with flour. Add yeast mixture and let set, covered, overnight.

* Will keep covered in fridge for 1 to 2 weeks.

Makes 3½ cups.

*Photo: Peggy's Cove is the most picturesque
and most photographed village in Canada.
It is also home to a hard-working fleet
of lobstermen.*

RYE BREAD

We think this glazed rye bread with its tangy buttermilk and flavorful molasses is a good breakfast bread, toasted and buttered.

2 cups	buttermilk	500 mL
½ cup	molasses	125 mL
¼ cup	butter	50 mL
2 tsp	salt	10 mL
1½ tsp	caraway seed	7 mL
2 tbsp	dry yeast	25 mL
½ cup	warm water	125 mL
1 tsp	granulated sugar	5 mL
1 cup	wheat germ	250 mL
2 cups	light rye flour	500 mL
3½–4½ cups	unbleached white flour	825–1125 mL
2 tbsp	vegetable oil	25 mL
1 tbsp	maple syrup	15 mL
2 tbsp	warm water	25 mL

In a saucepan, heat the buttermilk, molasses, butter, salt and caraway seed until the butter melts. Set aside to cool. In a small mixing bowl, dissolve dry yeast and sugar in warm water. Cover and let rise for 5 to 7 minutes or until the yeast is foamy. Add yeast mixture to cooled buttermilk mixture. Add the wheat germ and rye flour, stirring until well blended and smooth. Stir in unbleached flour, 1 cup at a time, until a stiff dough is formed and dough does not stick to sides of bowl. Flour a work surface with the rest of the unbleached flour and turn the dough onto it; cover with a damp cloth and let rest for 15 minutes.

Knead the dough for 5 to 10 minutes until smooth and elastic, then form dough into a ball. Place dough into a well-oiled bowl and turn to coat dough with oil. Cover and place in warm spot to rise for approximately 1 hour or until double in size. Punch the dough down and gently knead for 1 minute. Divide dough into 3 equal portions, form into 3 round loaves and place in a greased 9-inch (22-cm) round pan or on a baking sheet. Cover and let rise for 45 minutes.

Prepare glaze by combining maple syrup with warm water. Pierce the raised loaves all over with a fork and brush on the glaze. Bake in a preheated 375°F (190°C) oven for 35 to 45 minutes or until bread sounds hollow when tapped. Remove bread from pans and place on a wire rack to cool. While the bread is still hot, brush with remaining glaze.

Makes 3 loaves.

OLD-FASHIONED DINNER ROLLS

The kind of rolls that you would imagine being served at the farmhouse table or at a church supper. They are light and soft and great with a chowder.

2 cups	milk	500 mL
⅓ cup	shortening	75 mL
½ cup	granulated sugar	125 mL
1 tbsp	salt	15 mL
1	egg, lightly beaten	1
2 tbsp	dry yeast	25 mL
½ cup	warm water	125 mL
2 tsp	granulated sugar	10 mL
6-6½ cups	all-purpose flour	1500-1625 mL

In a small saucepan, scald milk over medium heat (heat milk until a thin film covers the surface; do not boil).

In a large mixing bowl, combine shortening, sugar, salt and beaten egg; add scalded milk and set aside to cool until lukewarm. In a small mixing bowl, dissolve dry yeast in warm water and sugar; set aside until yeast is foamy. Combine with shortening mixture, blending well. Add flour 1 cup (250 mL) at a time, until dough comes away clean from the sides of the bowl; knead until dough is smooth and elastic. Cover and set aside in a warm place to rise for 1 hour.

Punch dough down; knead until smooth. Form into balls and place on a greased baking pan. Brush with melted butter, cover and let rise until rolls are double in size, approximately 1 hour. Bake in a preheated 350°F (180°C) oven for 15 to 20 minutes or until the rolls are golden brown.

Makes 2 to 3 dozen good-sized rolls.

BARME BRACH BREAD

*Direct from Ireland to Nova Scotia. The Barme Brach, a Gaelic name
(which in English means speckled yeast bread), is a wonderful cake–like bread that is
delicious with coffee or tea. It was traditionally served on All–Saints Day, the day after
Halloween. The baker would wrap an odd assortment of items such as thimbles,
charms and coins in pieces of cloth and stir them right into the batter. Your future
could be predicted by the object found in your piece of bread. We've left them out
of this recipe, but they make a fun addition.*

3 cups	all- purpose flour	750 mL
¼ cup	granulated sugar	50 mL
1 tsp	salt	5 mL
1 tsp each	ground cinnamon, nutmeg and allspice	5 mL each
¼ cup	butter	50 mL
1¼ cup	warmed milk	300 mL
1 tbsp	granulated sugar	15 mL
1 tbsp	dry yeast	15 mL
2	eggs, beaten	2
	Grated rind of one lemon	
1⅓ cup	raisins	325 mL
⅔ cup	currants	150 mL
⅔ cup	candied fruit peel	150 mL
1½ tbsp	honey or granulated sugar	20 mL
3 tbsp	boiling water	45 mL

In a large mixing bowl, mix together flour, granulated sugar, salt, cinnamon, nutmeg
and allspice. Cut in the butter with the flour mixture. In a small mixing bowl, combine
¼ cup (50 mL) of the warmed milk with 1 tbsp (15 mL) granulated sugar and yeast;
let yeast rise until foamy. Combine the remaining 1 cup (250 mL) warmed milk with
beaten eggs in a small bowl; add to yeast mixture. Pour milk and yeast mixture into
dry ingredients. Beat with a wooden spoon or knead with your hands. The dough
should be stiff but elastic. Fold or knead in raisins, currants, fruit peel and lemon rind
(charms can be added at this time). Cover dough with tea towel and let rise in a warm
place for 30 to 60 minutes or until dough has doubled in size.

Punch dough down and knead for 3 to 5 minutes until smooth and elastic, shape into
a circle and place in a 10-inch (25-cm) greased round pan. Cover and let rise for
30 minutes or until dough has risen to the top of the pan. Bake in a preheated 350°F
(180°C) oven for 1 hour or until golden brown. Remove from oven and place on wire
rack to cool. Combine honey or sugar with boiling water to form glaze and brush on
bread while still warm.

Makes 1 loaf.

Preserves, Breakfast and Beverages

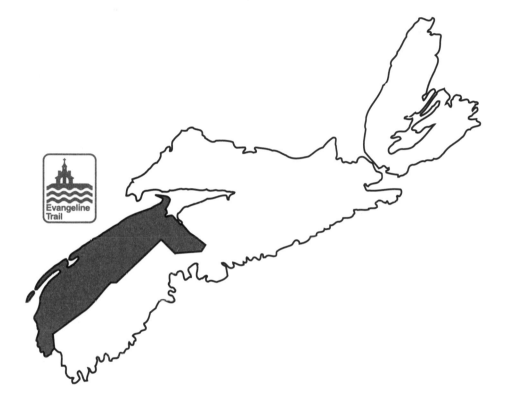

Evangeline
Trail

THE EVANGELINE TRAIL

SAMUEL DE CHAMPLAIN WAS A SMART MAN. HE LANDED IN SOUTHWESTERN Nova Scotia in 1604 with an exhausted crew, who were hungry for fresh food and sick of one another. What to do? In their settlement, or habitation, as it was called, Champlain set up the first social club in North America, calling it the Order of Good Cheer. The club was founded just before the winter set in and worked very well, lifting the spirits of the French explorers he had brought along. Champlain wrote, "We spent this winter very pleasantly and had good fare by means of the Order of Good Cheer which I established, and which everybody found beneficial to his health, and more profitable than all sorts of medicine we might have used. This order consisted of a chain which we used to place with certain little ceremonies about the neck of one of our people, commissioning him for that day to go hunting. The next day it was conferred upon another, and so on, in order. All vied with each other to see who could do the best, and bring back the finest game."

The habitation that Champlain founded was called Port Royal, and was built on the low-lying marshlands of the western shore, an area similar to the French homeland of the new settlers. The French spread out along the Annapolis River, which flowed through the warm, protected Annapolis Valley before entering the ocean in the Bay of Fundy. They were expert in reclaiming marshlands by the use of ingeniously designed dykes, which still function today.

The land that emerged when the sea was kept out is some of the most fertile farmland in Canada. It is the heart of Nova Scotia's fruit industry, and is covered in orchards producing apples, pears, peaches, plums and cherries.

During the 1600s and 1700s, the French and the newer English residents struggled for land and power, resulting in an agreement that the English would keep mainland Nova Scotia, known as Acadia, and the French would be allowed to claim Cape Breton Island. Although Cape Breton is beautiful, with great granite mountains dropping steeply to the sea that surrounds it, for farmers and fur traders it was not so inviting. The Port Royal people decided to stay where they were, saying they would remain neutral in the dispute. The English were not satisfied, however, and demanded that the French who remained swear an oath of allegiance, or leave. Most refused to take the oath, and in 1755 more than 10,000 Acadians were forced onto British ships and deported. They ended up spread out in Quebec, Louisiana, and even the West Indies. The Cajuns (or 'cadians) of Louisiana are the direct descendants of the deported Acadians, and the Cajun food which is so popular today has Nova Scotia roots. Longfellow immortalized the struggle, the sorrow and the deportation of the Acadians in his epic poem "Evangeline."

After years of fighting, some of the Acadians returned, finding New England Planters happily farming the vacated lands. The English soon increased their number by many thousands with the arrival of Loyalists who fled the American colonies during the days leading up to the American revolution.

Some of the French built new farms, but many turned to the sea, becoming the expert fishermen of the western shore. That tradition remains today. The main catches are herring, mackerel and cod. The most famous shellfish is the Digby scallop — its sweet, pearly white flesh is what all other scallops are judged by.

The Annapolis Valley is protected from the harshest weather by a mountain range separating the valley floor from the late spring and early fall winds blowing off the Bay of Fundy. The soil is rich and fertile and the average temperature is warmer here than anywhere else in the province. While crops of all kinds are grown here, apples predominate.

It was just sunset when we entered the Annapolis Valley, and we could clearly see Cape Blomidon, the sacred jut of land rising up from the ocean and protecting the valley. Cunard is a village that sits between the Cunard River and the North Mountain. The Cunard name is known around the world because of one wandering descendant, Samuel, whose urge to travel and desire for comfort gave birth to the Cunard Steamship Line, owner of the *Queen Elizabeth*, the *QE2*, the *Queen Mary* and the *Titanic*.

Peter Van Oostrum lives in Cunard, on a farm first established in 1768 by the Tuppers, a descendant of whom would later serve Canada as Prime Minister. Before the Tuppers arrived, the land was farmed by the French, who were obliged to give it up in the mid-eighteenth century. One area of Peter's farm is still called the French Orchard in honor of the original farmers.

We sat in the kitchen over coffee and apple cake and talked apples. "Our main crop is MacIntosh," Peter said, "but we also grow Cortlands, Northern Spys, Red Delicious and some varieties not seen much around here like Johnny Gold and Alstar." There happened to be a basket of Alstars next to the table and we found the fruit firm and sweet. There is a science to understanding the different characteristics of the apple varieties. Many cooks have been surprised when the crisp apples they use in an apple pie bake into applesauce.

Peter works closely with a local beekeeper, whose hives, an essential connection in ensuring good pollination of the trees, are situated in his orchard. They provide a supply of sweet apple blossom honey that teams so well with the apples in baked desserts.

"We have 10,000 trees in our nursery. We keep up with the new technologies and grow dwarf trees, experiment with different root stocks and grafting. The trees end up in our orchards and are also sold to other Valley farmers." We asked Peter the all-too-common question for the small family farmer: will the farm carry on in the future? His answer was heartening. "My wife and I have always had help from our six children. My two sons and one of my daughters still work the farm with us or have established their own farms. We now have ten grandchildren to carry on the tradition." After 200 years Cunard Orchards looks like it will be around for the long haul.

BEET RELISH

Relishes are old-fashioned condiments which are finding their way back to the cooking repertoire. They are somewhat time-consuming to prepare, because of the need to follow careful procedures in canning. However, they keep for a long time in the pantry, one batch makes several jars and they are a welcome gift. Many boxes of relish come with easy sterilizing instructions.

Beet relish is a beautiful ruby red that brings a burst of color to the plate. Chow Chow, with green tomatoes, is the ingenious way to use the inevitable store of tomatoes that didn't ripen fast enough to beat the frost.

Relishes are good with roasted meats, poultry and the "meatier" fish, like swordfish or shark.

4 lb	beets	2 kg
4	medium onions	4
1 lb	sweet red peppers	500 g
3 cups	white vinegar	750 mL
2 cups	granulated sugar	500 mL
2 tsp	salt	10 mL
2 tbsp	pickling spice	25 mL

Wash and peel the raw, uncooked beets and cut into chunks. Remove skins from onions and cut into pieces. Wash and remove seeds from red peppers; cut into pieces. In a food processor or food mill, put vegetables through using a coarse blade to produce a chunky mixture.

In a large saucepan over medium heat, combine vinegar, sugar and salt, stirring to dissolve sugar and salt. Bring to a boil. Add pickling spice, tied loosely in a cheesecloth bag. Add vegetables and boil gently for 30 minutes, stirring occasionally to prevent sticking. Remove the spice bag. Pour into sterilized jars or bottles immediately, and cover with tight-fitting lids.

Yields 12 cups (3 L).

CHOW CHOW

36	medium green tomatoes, sliced	36
3 lb	onions, peeled and sliced	1.5 kg
½ cup	coarse salt	125 mL
4 cups	apples, peeled, cored and chopped	1 L
3½ cups	granulated sugar	875 mL
2 cups	white vinegar	500 mL
¼ cup	pickling spice	50 mL

In a large bowl, alternate layers of sliced tomatoes and onions; sprinkle each layer lightly with coarse salt. Invert a plate on top of the vegetables, pressing firmly. Let stand overnight. In the morning, drain liquid, place mixture in a colander and rinse under cold running water, and then drain. In a large saucepan or soup pot, combine apples, sugar, vinegar and pickling spice (tied in a cheesecloth bag). Add tomatoes and onions. Bring to a boil, reduce heat and then allow to simmer, stirring occasionally, for approximately 30 minutes or until onions become translucent. Remove spice bag and pour immediately into sterilized jars and seal.

Makes approximately 16 cups (4 L).

CHUTNEY

Chutney refers to any number of preserved condiments which are made with fruits, vegetables and spices. While many chutneys are East Indian in origin they need not be made with Indian spices. They can be used as an accompaniment to almost any meat, fish or fowl.

All three of the recipes here allow you to take advantage of the surplus of summer vegetables and fruits that taste so good when freshly picked but can't all be used immediately. These chutneys will all keep for a long time in a cool pantry and lend an unexpected elegance to a simply prepared entrée. They also make wonderful gifts, especially handy when you get a last-minute invitation.

Tomato Chutney

6½ cups	ripe red tomato	1375 mL
6 cups	ripe tart apples, peeled, cored and diced	1250 mL
¾ cup	cider vinegar	75 mL
1 cup	granulated sugar	250 mL
½ cup	maple syrup	125 mL
1 tsp	pickling spice	5 mL
½ tsp	whole cloves	2 mL

Peel and dice tomatoes; press overnight. In the morning, pour off and discard the juice and add the tomato pulp to the diced apples. In a large stock pot, add vinegar, sugar, maple syrup and mix well. Add tomato and apple mixture to the stock pot.

Put pickling spice and cloves into a cheesecloth bag and add to mixture. Simmer, stirring occasionally, until thickened (about 15 minutes). Remove from heat, discard spice bag and pour chutney into hot, sterilized jars and seal.

Makes approximately 3 to 4 pints.

Dutch Vegetable Chutney

3	medium cucumbers, peeled, diced and seeded	3
2	medium zucchini, diced	2
1	small cabbage, shredded	1
½	red pepper, seeded and diced	½
½	green pepper, seeded and diced	½
1	cauliflower, chopped	1
1	broccoli (florets only), chopped	1
1	red onion, peeled and diced	1
2	medium carrots, peeled and diced	2
2 tbsp	salt (coarse)	25 mL
2½ cups	cider vinegar	625 mL
¼ cup	pickling spice	50 mL
¼ cup	all-purpose flour	50 mL
2 cups	granulated sugar	500 mL
1 tbsp	dry mustard	15 mL
2 tsp	tumeric	10 mL

Dice vegetables uniformly into small chunks and place in a large bowl; add salt and mix well. Press vegetables overnight. Drain well in morning or approximately 12 hours later.

In a large stockpot, combine vinegar and pickling spice which has been put into a cheesecloth bag. Allow to simmer for 1 hour, then remove bag of pickling spice. In separate bowl, sift together flour, sugar, dry mustard and tumeric. Add to vinegar and whisk until slightly thickened.

Combine vegetables and vinegar mixture in stock pot and simmer over low heat until vegetables are lightly cooked (20 to 25 minutes) but still firm. Remove from heat, then bottle in sterilized jars. May be stored in cool place for several months.

Delicious condiment for fish.

Makes approximately 4 to 5 12-oz (345-mL) jars.

Blueberry Chutney

8 cups	wild blueberries	2 L
1½ cups	golden seedless raisins	375 mL
1 cup	white vinegar	250 mL
1½ cups	brown sugar, packed	375 mL
1 cup	onions, peeled and finely chopped	250 mL
2 tbsp	orange zest	25 mL
1 tsp	dry mustard	5 mL
½ tsp	ground ginger	2 mL
½ tsp	ground cinnamon	2 mL
¼ tsp	salt	1 mL
pinch	cayenne pepper	pinch
pinch	nutmeg	pinch

In a large saucepan, combine all ingredients. Bring to a gentle boil and simmer for 20 minutes, stirring frequently. Remove about half the sauce and purée in food processor or blender, then return to saucepan and continue simmering, stirring frequently, until thickened, for about 20 minutes. Continue to stir for additional 5 minutes, if necessary, skimming foam as required. Pour into hot sterilized bottles. Seal and cool.

Makes 5 cups (1.25 L).

CAPE SMOKEY BLUEBERRY BUTTERMILK PANCAKES

Blueberries explode with flavor when cooked, and even frozen blueberries can conjure up the taste of summer. Add nutmeg, cinnamon and maple syrup to these pancakes and you'll have a real treat.

1⅔ cup	all-purpose flour	425 mL
1 tbsp	granulated sugar	15 mL
4 tsp	baking powder	20 mL
½ tsp	salt	2 mL
½ tsp	ground cinnamon	2 mL
¼ tsp	ground nutmeg	1 mL
4	large eggs separated	4
2¼ cups	buttermilk	550 mL
¼ tsp	cream of tartar	1 mL
¼ cup	butter, melted and cooled	50 mL
2 cups	wild blueberries, fresh or frozen (do not thaw)	500 mL

In a large mixing bowl, sift together flour, sugar, baking powder, salt, cinnamon and nutmeg. In a small bowl, beat the egg yolks and buttermilk until slightly blended. In a small mixing bowl, beat the egg whites until foamy, add the cream of tartar and continue to beat until soft peaks form. Add the egg yolk mixture to the flour mixture and mix lightly with a fork until flour is moistened. Stir in the melted butter. The batter should be lumpy as overmixing will toughen it. Fold in the egg whites with a rubber spatula. Lightly butter a preheated hot griddle or skillet. Spoon in batter and sprinkle blueberries on top. When pancake is golden brown on bottom and bubbles appear on surface, flip over and cook for 1 minute on the other side.

Makes 4 to 6 servings.

FRESH FRUIT PANCAKES

Sweet with honey and fragrant with cinnamon, these fruit-filled cakes are a change from plain or blueberry pancakes.

2	eggs	2
¼ cup	vegetable oil	50 mL
¼ cup	liquid honey	50 mL
¾ cup	plain yogurt	175 mL
½ cup	milk	125 mL
½ cup	apple juice	125 mL
1½ cup	all purpose flour	375 mL
1½ tsp	baking soda	7 mL
½ tsp	salt	2 mL
¼ tsp	ground cinnamon	1 mL
1	small apple, unpeeled, cored and finely chopped	1
1	small pear, unpeeled, cored and finely chopped	1

In a large mixing bowl, whisk together eggs, oil, honey, yogurt, milk and apple juice until well combined. In a small bowl, sift together flour, baking soda, salt and cinnamon. Fold in dry ingredients until blended, then stir in chopped fruit.

In a lightly oiled heavy-bottomed skillet over medium heat, place ½ cup (125 mL) of batter for each pancake. Cook on one side until bubbles appear on the surface, then carefully flip to the other side and continue to cook until golden. Serve with maple syrup.

Makes 7 to 8 servings.

MARGAREE VALLEY FRENCH TOAST

A brunch dish beyond adjectives, this French toast is made with Porridge Bread
(see page 130). If porridge bread is not available then use ½-inch (1-cm) thick slices of
another brown bread. We make it for Sunday dinner if brunch time slips away.

5	eggs	5
¼ cup	milk	50 mL
1 cup	rolled oats	250 mL
¼ cup	brown sugar	50 mL
1 tsp	cinnamon	5 mL
6 to 8	slices of porridge bread	6 to 8
	Butter as required for cooking	

In a medium-sized bowl, whisk together eggs and milk. In a pie plate, combine oats, brown sugar and cinnamon. In a skillet, melt butter until bubbly. Dip both sides of porridge bread in egg mixture and then coat both sides with spiced oatmeal. Sauté in butter until golden. Serve with maple syrup.

Makes 3 to 4 servings.

HONEY BUTTER

A simple but delightful spread for bread, crackers, toast,
French toast, hot biscuits and pancakes.

1 cup	butter or margarine	250 mL
1½ cups	liquid honey	375 mL

Cream butter and gradually add honey. Refrigerate between uses.

STRATA

Here is another dish that shows the Italian influence on Nova Scotian cooking. Strata makes a perfect brunch buffet dish, since the work is done the day before it is served. This is a good way to use up some of the basil from the herb garden.

1 cup	milk	250 mL
½ cup	dry vermouth	125 mL
1	loaf, day-old French bread	1
1 cup	fresh basil, washed	250 mL
3 tbsp	olive oil	45 mL
½ lb	back bacon, thinly sliced	250 g
3	ripe tomatoes, sliced	3
1 lb	herb cream cheese or smoked salmon–flavored cream cheese (in the absence of herb cream cheese make your own with plain cream cheese and snipped chives creamed together)	500 g
4	large eggs, beaten	4
	Salt and pepper	
½ cup	whipping cream	125 mL

On the day before serving, combine the milk and vermouth in a bowl. Slice the bread into ½-inch (1-cm) slices and dip a few at a time in the milk mixture. Remove bread and gently squeeze out as much liquid as possible, trying not to tear bread in the process.

Cover the bottom of an oval gratin dish or a rectangular baking dish with a single layer of the bread strips. Rub the fresh basil leaves with the olive oil and cut into strips. Place some of the basil leaves, bacon, tomato slices and cream cheese on top of the bread. Continue layering bread and rest of the ingredients until all are used. Pour the beaten eggs, seasoned with salt and pepper, over the top and cover with plastic wrap. Refrigerate overnight.

The following morning, remove from refrigerator 1 hour before serving time. Preheat oven to 350°F (180°C). Pour the whipping cream over the dish, covering evenly, and bake for 50 to 60 minutes or until top is golden brown.

Makes 6 servings.

TRADITIONAL FISHCAKES

Fishcakes with salt cod, potatoes and herbs are a good breakfast or brunch dish.
They can be served alone, but are nice accompanied by poached eggs. Here are two
recipes which prove that an old traditional recipe can indeed become new.
Fishcakes can be made in large batches and frozen.

1 lb	salt cod	500 g
2½ lb	potatoes, peeled and cut into chunks	1 kg
3	onions, peeled and chopped	3
½ cup	salt pork	125 mL
¼ cup	white vinegar	50 mL
1 cup	whipping cream	250 mL
2	eggs, slightly beaten	2
1 tsp	pepper	5 mL
1 tsp	summer savory	5 mL

Soak codfish in water overnight or for at least 3 hours, then drain. In a saucepan, cook the potatoes in boiling water until tender. About 10 minutes after the potatoes start to cook, add the codfish and continue to cook until potatoes are done. Drain, and mash cod and potatoes together.

In a skillet over medium heat, sauté the onions with salt pork, which has been cut into small pieces. In a bowl, combine the vinegar and the whipping cream. Add cream mixture to the onion and pork; simmer until whipping cream is reduced by half. Add cream mixture to potato and cod mixture, along with the eggs, pepper and summer savory. Mix well. Shape into fishcake patties and pan fry in a small amount of butter until golden brown. These freeze well for future use.

Makes 18 medium-sized fishcakes.

CONTEMPORARY FISHCAKES AND LEMON BUTTER SAUCE

½ lb	dry salt cod	250 g
1½ lbs	potatoes, peeled and diced	750 g
¼ lb	finely diced salt pork	125 g
½ cup	onions, peeled and finely diced	125 mL
½ cup	celery, finely diced	125 mL
½ tsp	fresh thyme	2 mL
½ tsp	dried summer savory	2 mL
1 tsp	fresh chives, chopped	5 mL

Lemon Butter Sauce:

⅔ cup	white wine	175 mL
1½ tsp	shallots, chopped	7 mL
1 tbsp	lemon juice, freshly squeezed	15 mL
⅔ cup	whipping cream	175 mL
1 cup	unsalted butter	250 mL
	Salt and pepper to taste	

Soak salt cod in water overnight. Drain fish and place in a saucepan of water over medium heat, bring to a boil, reduce heat and simmer until fish is tender and flaky, approximately 15 minutes. Taste fish partway through cooking process and, if it is still salty, drain and start again with fresh water. Break cod into small pieces. In another saucepan, cook potatoes in sufficient water to cover until tender. Drain and mash. In a skillet, sauté the salt pork until the fat is rendered out and pieces start to turn white. Add the onions and celery, cooking until the onions are almost translucent. Remove from heat, stir in the thyme, summer savory and chives. Add salt cod and sautéed vegetables to mashed potatoes; stir to combine. Add some of the rendered pork fat to the potato and fish mixture, being careful not to add too much – this will make the mixture soggy. Season with salt and pepper and let cool. Form into fishcakes. Pan fry on griddle until golden brown.

Lemon butter sauce: In a saucepan over medium heat, add wine, shallots and lemon juice; reduce slightly. Add cream and reduce another 5 minutes. Cut butter into cubes and add slowly to the cream mixture over medium heat, whisking until a smooth sauce is obtained. Season to taste.

Serve fishcakes with the warm lemon butter sauce drizzled over top.

Makes 12 medium-sized fishcakes.

POACHED EGGS WITH SMOKED SALMON

4.

The addition of silky smoked salmon, our famous worldwide export,
gives these eggs a distinctively Nova Scotian taste.

4	English muffins	4
8	eggs	8
8	slices smoked N.S. salmon	8
	(approx. ¼ lb or 125 g)	

Hollandaise Sauce:

3	egg yolks	3
2 tbsp	lemon juice	25 mL
⅔ cup	butter	150 mL
	Salt	
	Pinch of cayenne pepper (optional)	

To make Hollandaise sauce: You will need a double boiler or medium saucepan that will accommodate a metal bowl. Place egg yolks in top of double boiler or metal bowl over hot but not boiling water. Whisk in 1 tbsp (15 mL) of lemon juice and 1 tbsp (15 mL) of the butter until butter is melted. Whisk in remaining butter about 2 tbsp (25 mL) at a time until it is all melted and sauce begins to thicken. Add the remaining lemon juice, salt and cayenne pepper to taste. Continue heating until the sauce is thick and smooth. Keep sauce warm but do not overcook.

Toast and butter the English muffins. Set one muffin on each plate. Place one slice of smoked salmon on each muffin half.

Poach eggs.

Place one egg on each muffin half and spoon Hollandaise sauce on top.

Makes 4 servings.

Hot Mulled Apple Cider

Mulled cider has many variations. Ours is simple and highlights the apple. Perfect for the festive season.

8 cups	apple cider	2 L
1 cup	brown sugar	250 mL
⅓ cup	butter	75 mL
1-2	cinnamon sticks	1-2
6	whole cloves	6

In a large saucepan, bring apple cider to a gentle boil. Add brown sugar, butter, cinnamon and cloves; reduce heat and simmer until sugar dissolves and flavors have blended.

As an alternative, rum or brandy may be added.

Makes 8 to 10 servings.

HOT BLUENOSE PUNCH

This hot beverage is just right after a fall or winter day outdoors or for a holiday party.
Fragrant with blueberries and rich with sweet spices, Bluenose Punch
is an unusual and warming drink.

1 cup	blueberry syrup (see below)	250 mL
2 cups	water	500 mL
2 cups	apple cider or apple juice	500 mL
¼ cup	liquid honey or maple syrup	50 mL
2 tbsp	lemon juice	25 mL
1 tsp	ground allspice	5 mL
4	whole cloves	4
2	cinnamon sticks	2
15	lemon slices (optional)	15

In a large saucepan combine all the above ingredients. Bring to a boil, reduce heat and simmer for 2 to 3 minutes. Serve hot, garnished with a lemon slice. As an option add 8 oz (250 mL) rum or vodka to punch just before serving.

Makes 10 ½-cup (125-mL) servings.

Blueberry Syrup:

4 cups	fresh or frozen wild blueberries	1 L
⅓ cup	water	75 mL
1½ cup	granulated sugar	375 mL
¼ cup	lemon juice	50 mL

In a large saucepan, combine all the above ingredients and bring to a boil. Reduce heat and simmer for 10 to 15 minutes. Remove from heat and cool. Strain off pulp by using a fine sieve, strainer or cheesecloth. Cover and refrigerate syrup.

Makes 2 cups (500 mL).

RHUBARB PUNCH

An interesting combination of tart rhubarb and sweet juices.

2 lb	fresh or frozen rhubarb, cut in cubes	1 kg
2½ cups	water	625 mL
1 cup	granulated sugar	250 mL
2 cups	unsweetened pineapple juice	500 mL
¼ cup	lemon juice, freshly squeezed	50 mL
4 cups	ginger ale or lemon-lime pop	1 L

Combine rhubarb and water in a saucepan. Cook over medium heat until the rhubarb becomes soft and starts to break apart, approximately 10 to 15 minutes. Strain the rhubarb mixture through a fine strainer or sieve, collecting the liquid in a bowl, and chill rhubarb juice. Add sugar, pineapple juice and lemon juice, stirring until sugar is dissolved. Just before serving, add ginger ale or lemon-lime pop.

Makes 12 cups (3 L).

FRESH MINT TEA AND APPLE CIDER

A fantastic non-alcoholic refresher, this drink combines apple, mint, rosemary and tea for an unusual and unforgettable drink.

4 cups	sweet apple cider	1 L
4 cups	water	1 L
2	Earl Grey tea bags	2
3	apple spice tea bags	3
3	mint tea bags	3
1	sprig fresh rosemary	1
10	fresh mint leaves	
10	strawberries, sliced	10

In saucepan, combine cider, water, tea bags and rosemary sprig; bring to a boil. Remove from heat and let steep for 10 minutes. Strain, pressing to extract all liquid. Chill and serve in iced glasses, garnished with a mint leaf and a slice of strawberry.

Makes 8 to 10 servings.

Index